THIS BOOK
BELONGS TO ...

100%
UNOFFICIAL

First published in Great Britain 2023 by 100% Unofficial,
a part of Farshore

An imprint of HarperCollins*Publishers*
1 London Bridge Street, London SE1 9GF
www.farshore.co.uk

HarperCollins*Publishers*
Macken House, 39/40 Mayor Street Upper,
Dublin 1 D01 C9W8
Ireland

Written by Daniel Lipscombe
Illustrations by Matt Burgess

This book is an original creation by Farshore
© 2023 Farshore

ISBN 978 0 00 853715 9
Printed and bound in UAE
1

ONLINE SAFETY FOR YOUNGER FANS

Spending time online is great fun! Here are a few simple rules to help younger
fans stay safe and keep the internet a great place to spend time.

• Never give out your real name – don't use it as your username.
• Never give out any of your personal details.
• Never tell anybody which school you go to or how old you are.
• Never tell anybody your password, except a parent or guardian.
• Be aware that you must be 13 or over to create an account on many sites. Always check
the site policy and ask a parent or guardian for permission before registering.
• Always tell a parent or guardian if something is worrying you.

Stay safe online. Any website addresses listed in this book are correct at the
time of going to print. However, Farshore is not responsible for content hosted by
third parties. Please be aware that online content can be subject to change and
websites can contain content that is unsuitable for children. We advise that
all children are supervised when using the internet.

This book is produced from independently certified FSC™ paper
to ensure responsible forest management.

For more information visit: www.harpercollins.co.uk/green

ROBLOX
ANNUAL 2024

CONTENTS

HELLO!

WELCOME TO THE
2024 UNOFFICIAL ROBLOX ANNUAL!

We've got so many games to talk about this year. There are a few old favourites, plus some amazing new games. Roblox is so huge that we can't fit it all in 72 pages, but we'll look at lots of brilliant games. So, what will we be checking out this time?

In our tour around Roblox, we'll be dashing through a few obbys, speeding around in vehicles and trying desperately to survive.

We've got plenty for the tycoons out there, and lots for the players who like to be spooked and scared. If you prefer your games without any frights, there's still plenty of action-packed games to see.

No matter which games we're looking at, our focus is on the enjoyment we can get out of it. That's what Roblox is all about ... fun!

Get your game loaded, dress your avatar in your favourite outfit and accessories, and get ready to see some games you can play right now. There are games to play on your own, but also some to enjoy with your friends and family.

Ready?

HERE WE GO!

WE LOVE COLLECTING PETS

Roblox has heaps of games that allow you to collect pets. There are hundreds of places where you can buy eggs and hatch incredibly cute creatures. They can tag along while you role-play, or help you earn more in a tycoon game. We love pets!

ADOPT ME!

The most popular pet-collecting game just gets better and better every year. We can't stop playing, because we just want all the pets, then their neon versions and the mega-neon versions! Don't forget to check in with the game whenever Christmas or another celebration rolls around for exclusive special pets.

Dog
Pre-Teen

PET SIMULATOR X

Before buying any of the pets in Pet Simulator X, you'll need to spend time saving up coins by completing tasks. These allow you to not only buy more lovable pets, but also unlock new biomes for to explore with them. Some biomes, such as the volcano, will cost 50 million coins. Where you go next is up to you – where will you choose?

OBBY GAMES

Obby games can be some of the most fun experiences on Roblox. There's plenty of dangers to run away from and avoid. Sometimes you'll be escaping, sometimes just testing out your skills by moving through obstacles. There are lots of challenges to beat. LET'S GET RUNNING!

COTTON OBBY

Let's warm up with a nice easy obby. Cotton Obby is full of lovely, calming colours and straightforward obstacles. You won't be leaping from moving platforms or dodging speeding blocks here. This is a great obby to start out with if you're worried about others being too difficult.

There are a great variety of obstacles to try out and each one will train you to get better. While Cotton Obby is easier than most, it can sometimes be tricky. You might be hopping along happily, then suddenly the platform you're stood on will vanish. Be alert!

Thankfully, there are lots of checkpoints which save your progress along the way. You can even skip any sections that are holding you back. Overall, Cotton Obby looks rather calm and friendly, which suits this game perfectly. A great starting obby!

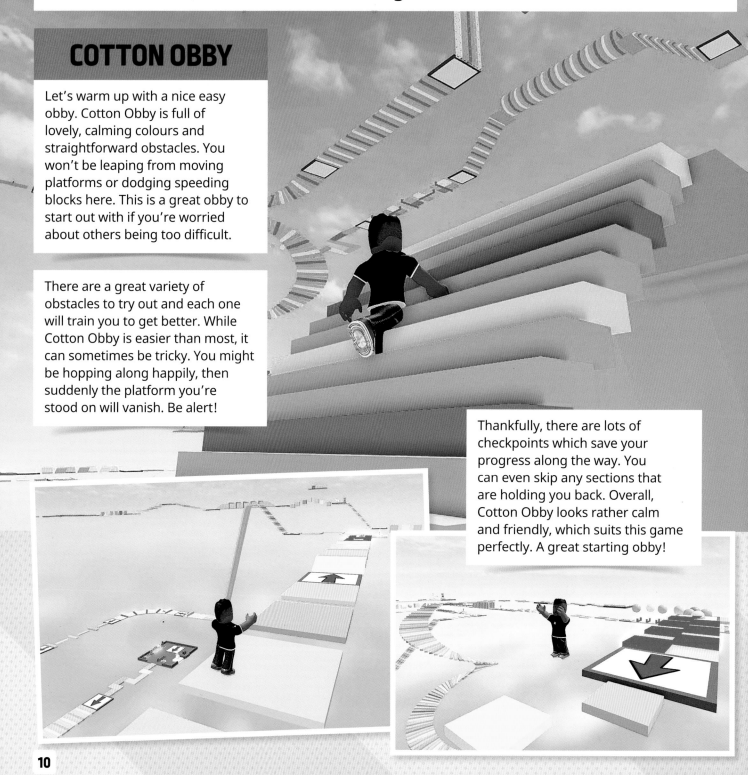

BARRY'S PRISON RUN!

There are a lot of obby games that have a theme or a place to escape. Barry's Prison Run! is a great example of this. You start out as a prisoner shut in a cell, and the goal is to follow an escape route to get out. What's great about this obby is the design. It's like escaping a real building designed by pros.

You'll be jumping off pipes, scurrying through tunnels, leaping over craters of lava. Nobody said escape would be easy! As with so many obby games, you'll be playing while other players try to escape too. So if you find an obstacle difficult, you have the option to watch how they do it before attempting to copy their success.

It's not just obstacles in Barry's Prison Run! There are plenty of angry guards who chase you down as you try to line up jumps. It's chaotic, fun and challenging. If you want to show off your skills or face a challenge, then start escaping!

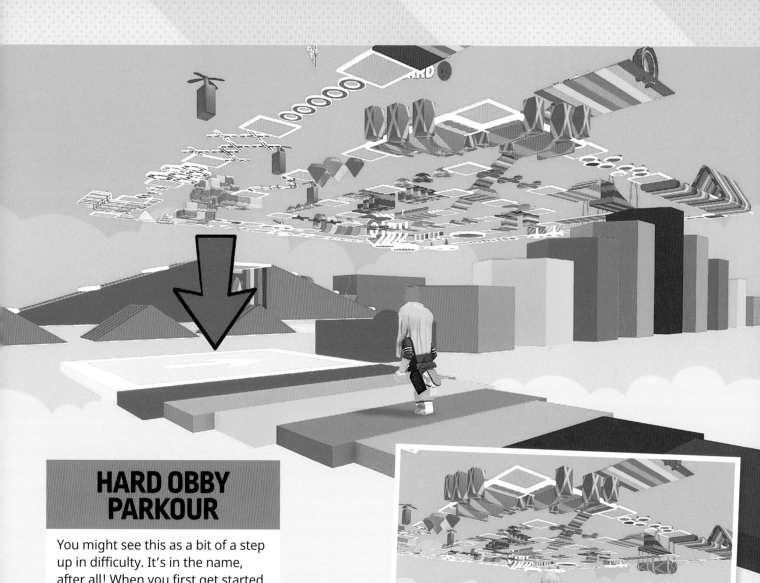

HARD OBBY PARKOUR

You might see this as a bit of a step up in difficulty. It's in the name, after all! When you first get started with Hard Obby Parkour, the opening obstacles are super easy. You might even wonder how this is supposed to be hard. However, it gets more difficult as you progress.

The jumps become longer and higher, so don't be surprised if you brush up against a danger block and fall to pieces. Literally. Although this looks very much like a simple obby, you will need to take some of the obstacles slowly to ensure you finish them intact.

Of course, Hard Obby Parkour is designed for everyone to try and play. With so many different shapes and sizes of platforms, it can be tricky to work out where to jump, but when you add in all the climbing sections, this obby absolutely rules!

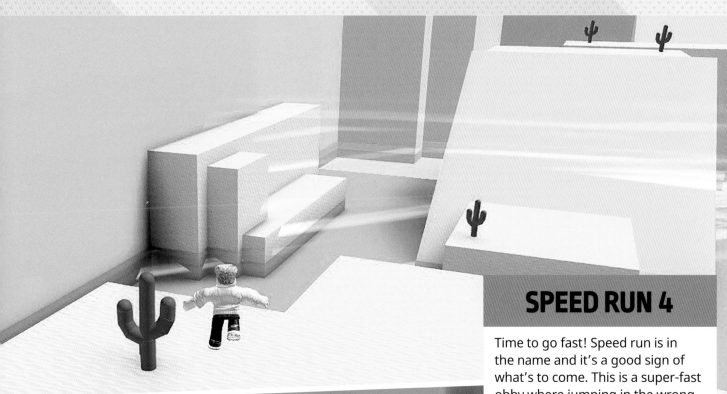

SPEED RUN 4

Time to go fast! Speed run is in the name and it's a good sign of what's to come. This is a super-fast obby where jumping in the wrong direction means falling into a pit and going all the way back to the start. You'll notice here that your little avatar runs like mad, and you need to time your jumps perfectly, often without knowing what's coming next.

You can still take your time on some of these jumps – but where's the fun in that. We recommend going as fast as possible and learning the jumps and obstacles as they come up.

One of the best things about Speed Run 4 is the design of the courses. They all look so different and that makes each level feel new. The same goes for the obstacles, too – there are wonky platforms, tiny safe zones to hop along and huge jumps that will require all your skill and speed to land.

There are over 30 levels to play through and you can collect rubies along the way to boost up your score. If you find a level is too tough to beat? Skip it!

ESCAPE THE CARNIVAL OF TERROR OBBY!

A lot like escaping a prison, escaping a carnival of terror means lots of scary and dangerous areas. While escaping this carnival, you'll face bottomless pits filled with teeth, spinning saw blades and terrifying clowns!

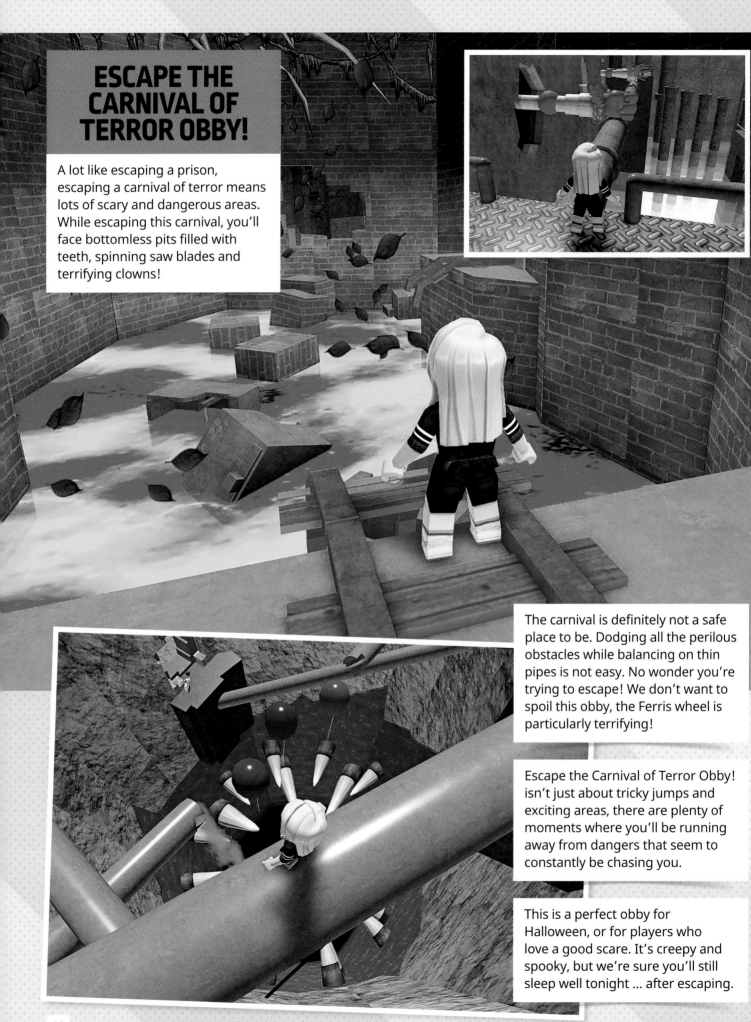

The carnival is definitely not a safe place to be. Dodging all the perilous obstacles while balancing on thin pipes is not easy. No wonder you're trying to escape! We don't want to spoil this obby, the Ferris wheel is particularly terrifying!

Escape the Carnival of Terror Obby! isn't just about tricky jumps and exciting areas, there are plenty of moments where you'll be running away from dangers that seem to constantly be chasing you.

This is a perfect obby for Halloween, or for players who love a good scare. It's creepy and spooky, but we're sure you'll still sleep well tonight ... after escaping.

FIVE TOP TIPS

1 GO SLOWLY

Unless you're playing a game where speed is important, there's no rush to beat any obby. Try going slowly and take your time lining up jumps. You're more likely to land on that tricky platform if you sit back and plan it.

2 ZOOM OUT

Across PC, console and mobile, there are ways to zoom out the view of your avatar. Take advantage of this, because it allows you to see more of the area and the obstacles. This is very important for speed-running games where you need to act fast.

3 TEST IT OUT

We all secretly love it when our Roblox avatar falls to pieces when touching a dangerous obstacle. It's pretty funny, every time. Don't be afraid of checking which parts of the obstacle will send you back to the checkpoint. You'll find the right route and get to laugh at the broken avatar.

4 WATCH OTHERS

If you're really struggling with a jump or obstacle, watch how other people tackle it. Most obby games will have other people playing nearby. You can use this to your advantage. See how they jump or what their route is through dangerous blocks. Then you'll make it too!

5 EASY > HARD

There are lots of obbys available on Roblox and most of them tell you if they will be easy or difficult. Take the obbys step-by-step and start off with easy. If you go straight to the hard stages, you might become disheartened when you can't manage them. Get that practice in on the easy obbys first.

TEN OF THE GREATEST
ROBLOX VEHICLES

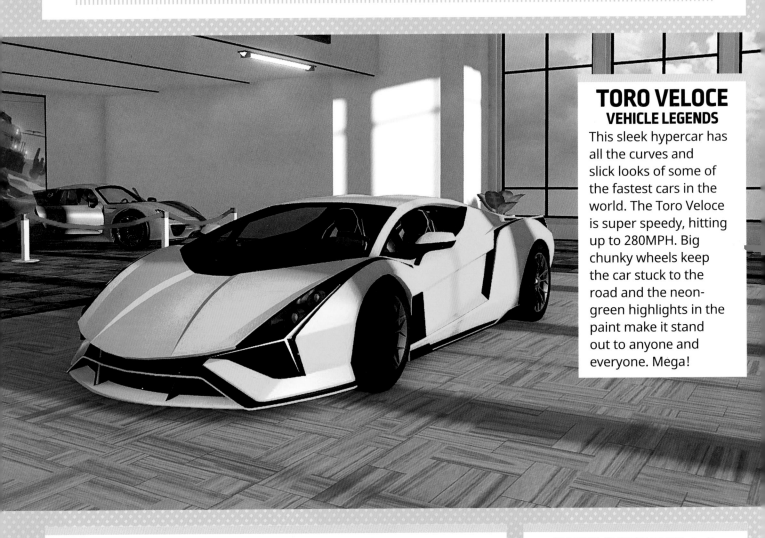

TORO VELOCE
VEHICLE LEGENDS

This sleek hypercar has all the curves and slick looks of some of the fastest cars in the world. The Toro Veloce is super speedy, hitting up to 280MPH. Big chunky wheels keep the car stuck to the road and the neon-green highlights in the paint make it stand out to anyone and everyone. Mega!

2012 BENLI SUPER YACHT
DRIVING EMPIRE

You need to have earned a fair chunk of in-game cash in order to buy this super yacht. Of course, it has plenty of rooms and several floors with places to eat and drink. There's also a helipad near the bow, just in case you want to store your helicopter. It will only cost you $50,000,000!

CHEVION BELLA
CAR DEALERSHIP TYCOON

If you want to drive around in a classic car, you have to choose the Chevion Bella. It looks like it just rolled out of an old movie, with white tyres, a large bumper and a vintage red paint job.

FIRE ENGINE
BERRY AVENUE RP

There's nothing stylish about this fire engine. It's a big boxy vehicle that doesn't go fast and is tough to turn tight corners. But it's so different to many other vehicles. Who wouldn't want to try it?!

2123 STALLION HOVER
ULTIMATE DRIVING

Whenever people wonder what the future will hold, many hope that flying cars will be a reality. There's something very cool about having the wheels replaced by turbine engines, that make the car take off from the road. This is the future. The possibilities are absolutely endless!

DHC-6 TWIN OTTER
PILOT TRAINING FLIGHT SIMULATOR

A plane that can land or take off on water is very cool indeed. The larger airliners are fun too, but they can't land on a lake, can they?! This can land anywhere!

TANK
BROOKHAVEN

Brookhaven is known for its super-deep role-playing. It's a nice quiet town filled with other players, working jobs or hanging out. So a tank is a bit over the top – but we love it!

AVANTA ZA15
CAR CRUSHERS 2

Formula One cars are not only some of the fastest cars around, but they look cool too. While there are other games on Roblox where you can drive an F1 car, here you can crush one!

MEGA BOX

Okay, so this car isn't flashy, and it isn't fast. In fact, it's pretty ridiculous. Which is why we love it! Imagine playing with your friends and they all choose supercars or classic convertibles and you arrive driving this!

1998 SENTINEL PARLIAMENT LIMO
GREENVILLE

Just how are these cars supposed to turn corners? They're so long, they can often fit more than twelve people inside. You'll usually see a limo either full of people heading to a party or prom, or it will be for a celebrity. It may not be the fastest, or the flashiest, but everyone will notice a limousine.

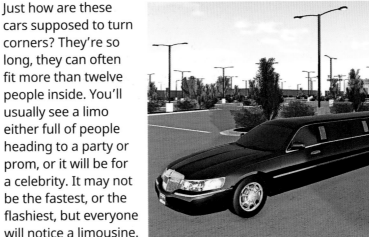

SURVIVAL GAMES

Survival games are huge on Roblox. Most players have tried one at least once. They can be scary, making you either run from a monster or play as one, or they can put you in a team and you have to solve puzzles to escape a situation. There's something exciting about trying to run away from danger!

PIGGY

Will you play as Piggy or as a survivor? If you're playing as the monstrous pig, your goal is to capture the survivors at any cost. You can make them jump by waiting in quiet corners or give chase and speed after them while they run for their lives!

Playing as a survivor needs a bit more skill. There are lots of puzzles to solve and moments where you must work with other players to escape. This happens by finding certain keys or tools. Communication via the chat box is very helpful because people may be asking for some of those tools you've collected.

Piggy plays over lots of chapters to create a thrilling story. In fact, there's a lot going on in Piggy when you add in all the maps, game modes and story chapters. Try to survive as long as possible to earn Piggy tokens. These allow you to unlock extra skins to play as new and different characters.

DOORS

Doors is a mega-popular horror game that everyone is playing. Played across one floor of a mysterious hotel, Doors sees players speeding around trying to escape the area by making it to door 100. It sounds simple, but there are monsters between you and your freedom.

These monsters, known as entities, roam the hotel freely. They will try anything to stop your escape and they come in different forms. Screech will appear behind you saying 'pssst' and you must stare into its eyes or it will attack you. Rush will flicker the lights, giving you only a short time to hide in a wardrobe, while it growls and stomps around looking for you. There are plenty more who will try to scare you by jumping out when you least expect it.

The only way to make it through each door is to hide or run. Getting past each area and through the doors sometimes just takes skill, but often requires a tool to help. Much like other games, you can work with different players to help each other escape to door 100.

EVADE

Evade is played in first-person view. This means you see out of your avatar's eyes, rather than from behind their body. For the first 30 seconds of Evade, you must quickly explore the area and hide. Once that time runs out, you'll be joined by Nextbots who chase around the map creating scary noises that will make you glad that you're hiding!

Weirdly, these bots are just a still image, but if anything, that makes them a bit creepier. They slide around making a lot of noise trying to catch you. If they do, you'll be knocked to the ground and you'll only be able to crawl. Another player may be able to revive you, but that puts them in a lot of danger. Standing still in Evade often means getting caught by one of the nasty Nextbots.

Don't worry, you aren't always left to your own devices. There are also lots of helpful items to give you a chance to escape. The radar is a great way to stay away from the Nextbots, and the decoy can make it harder for them to find you.

If you can complete the map without dying or needing to be revived, you'll earn cash and experience (EXP) to be used in the game's shop. Can you survive?

20

RAINBOW FRIENDS

Chapter one of Rainbow Friends puts you in a group of players going on a field trip to an amusement park called Odd World. On the way, the bus crashes and players are dragged off, only to wake up in a strange building where they have to help each other to escape some monsters.

Rainbow Friends is very popular because of its monsters, which are named after their colour: Blue, Green, Orange, Purple and Red. Each of them look different – some might even look friendly – but they are all trying to catch you.

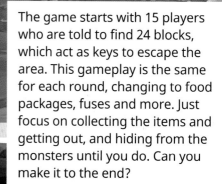

The game starts with 15 players who are told to find 24 blocks, which act as keys to escape the area. This gameplay is the same for each round, changing to food packages, fuses and more. Just focus on collecting the items and getting out, and hiding from the monsters until you do. Can you make it to the end?

CREATURE CHAOS

There are two sides to this survival game, and they're as different as night and day! You must take on the role of playing as a human survivor or as a creature and the action takes place in two stages – a day cycle and a night cycle, which both last for seven minutes.

All players spend the day cycle creating create safe spaces. These consist of defensive structures made of blocks and other building materials they can collect through the day cycle. If you're wondering what for, just wait until the night cycle – when half the players will be turned into creatures.

If, when night begins, you find yourself playing as a creature, you must try to reach and attack the players by any means necessary. The creatures are made of explosive materials, so you must use those powers to topple towers and bring down any structures built by players.

Eventually, creatures will find their way to the players, whether they've fallen to the ground or are hiding in their buildings. Once you have them in sight, it's time to go boom and eliminate them. Whether you're a human or a creature, teamwork is key to thriving in this game.

SURVIVAL GAMES
FIVE TOP TIPS

1 **DON'T WORRY IF YOU'RE CAUGHT**
Being caught in these games is all part of it. Sometimes, playing lots of short and quick games can allow you to learn the maps or find new hiding places. So, if you get caught quickly, try to work out what you learned in that round.

2 **HIDING IS SOMETIMES YOUR BEST BET**
Hiding can be just as helpful as running away. After all, if you've managed to hide, then you're still alive and will be ready to try escaping. Some players will keep running around, but that usually makes opposition players notice you.

3 **AS A MONSTER, STICK TO ONE PERSON**
If you're playing as the monster in any of these games, it's best to stick to hunting one player at a time. If you get distracted and hurry after another one, you'll let the player get away. Work through them one by one and don't stop until you catch them all.

4 **LEARN THE TOOLS**
Learn what each tool does and how they can help you escape. If you know where each item is used, and you've learned the map, you'll soon be speeding through each one. This also makes you valuable to the other players as they might need you to help them out.

5 **PLAY AS A TEAM**
In many survival games, you'll have to play on your own, trying to make it to another round first. In some, you'll need to play as a team. Use the chat box with your friends, to plan where you're moving to or announce what items you currently have. Working together can really help!

KEEP ON CLICKING

Clickers are the latest game type to take Roblox by storm. The games start off with you clicking your mouse or tapping a button as fast as you can to build up speed, or money, or materials. Then you use these to win races, buy new pets or become more powerful. Let's get clicking!

CLICKER SIMULATOR

Your thousands of clicks will take you to far-flung worlds – lands of fire, ice and magic – along with your adorable pets. Clicking here builds up both clicks and gems, each of which can be used to grow a great collection of pets. And those pets aren't only lovely to look at, each of them help you score more clicks! Can you bank enough clicks to climb to the top of the leaderboard?

MAX SPEED

You know when an athlete is waiting on the blocks at the start of a race? That is what you find yourself doing in Max Speed, except you need to click as much as possible to build up your speed for the race. Once the gate drops, off you go in a frantic dash to the finish line. You can earn race rewards and use them to buy upgrades, which will make you go faster and faster. Soon, your opponents will only see you as a fast blur!

MINING CLICKER SIMULATOR

We're not sure how Mining Clicker Simulator pulls materials out of thin air, but we won't ask too many questions. Click or tap to swing a pickaxe in the air and from this you'll be rewarded with new materials, which can be spent on tools or cute pets to make clicking even more fun!

FIVE OF THE BEST
TYCOON GAMES

It's pretty obvious what you'll be building in each of these great tycoon games. It's in the title! Most often with tycoon games though, the main goal isn't the only activity. There can be extra tasks and rewards, which provide products for your shops, theme parks or restaurant.

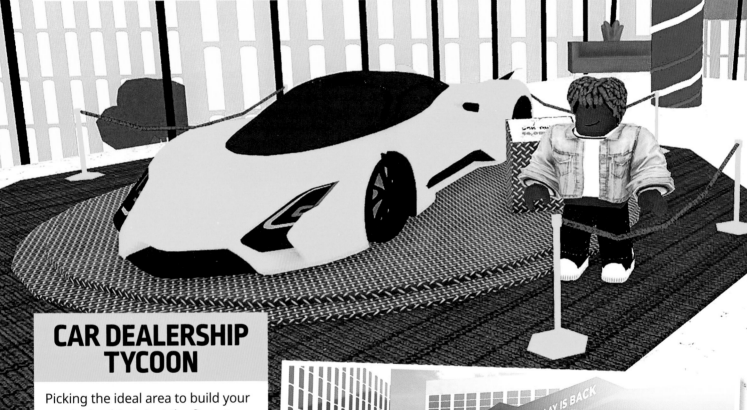

CAR DEALERSHIP TYCOON

Picking the ideal area to build your car dealership is just the first step in a long line of tasks. You can choose a style of building, then a patch of land where it will be built. You'll find yourself low on cash pretty much straight away, but have no fear, all it takes is a spot of driving to earn some more money.

It really is that simple. Just hop into a car – you start with one or two – then drive around the city. The more driving you do, the more you'll earn. You can earn extra cash for taking part in races against other players, which makes it even more fun.

Once your bank balance is healthier, head back to the dealership where you can choose further options to develop your building. Now, you can begin putting cars up for sale to make even more money. How you choose to run your dealership is totally up to you!

THEME PARK TYCOON 2

What's better than going to a theme park? Building one, right? You get to pick and choose which rides you want to build. You can say where the food and drink stalls go. And once the money starts coming in, you can even build a rollercoaster from scratch, choosing every twist and turn.

There is so much to do in Theme Park Tycoon 2! You can customise your park to create lots of themed areas for visitors to explore. There are trees, paths, fences, props, and you can even raise or lower the land to create hills and valleys. Everything can be changed in some way, so if you don't like the look of the drinks stall, just change the colours!

MEGA MANSION TYCOON

Mega Mansion Tycoon is a super-simple tycoon, probably best for those players who have never played a tycoon before. Your goal is to build a huge mansion that everybody would want to live in. Your money is earned as a slow trickle, constantly filling the mailbox at the front of your land.

In order to build the mansion, you control your avatar and walk them over big buttons. This places pieces of the mansion or furniture inside. For example, the first wall you place will cost a few hundred dollars. Later sections cost thousands, so everything gets built slowly. As you place the objects, the money in your mailbox grows faster. Before you know it, you'll be earning loads!

27

SMOOTHIE FACTORY TYCOON

Who knew you could sell smoothies for so much money?! In Smoothie Factory Tycoon, you're in charge of a factory that blends, processes and bottles up tasty-looking fruit drinks. There's a lot more to do here than on some other tycoon games. Upgrading your fruit blenders is only the beginning!

At first, you'll only be able to make strawberry smoothies, but it doesn't take long to unlock new fruit, such as oranges and bananas. You'll make money when the smoothies go out for delivery, and this profit can be used to upgrade your factory machines. Once you've been playing for some time, you will be able to automate different tasks so you won't be as busy.

RESTAURANT TYCOON 2

The first thing to decide in Restaurant Tycoon 2 is the name of your business. The next important step is to choose what cuisine you will serve. For example, Italian is pizza and pasta, Japanese is sushi and ramen, but what will your restaurant serve? Maybe a mix of cuisines from around the world?

Much like Smoothie Factory Tycoon, this tycoon game will have you doing a lot more than pressing buttons. It's your job to not only create a restaurant, but to also cook the meals and serve customers. That is until you have enough money to hire a chef and waiting staff. In fact, once you've been playing for a while, you'll have enough cash to upgrade everything.

TYCOON GAMES
FIVE TOP TIPS

1 **LEARN THE MONEY MAKING**
Most tycoon games have a few ways to make money. It may be from driving round a city or making lots of products and selling them quickly. Money equals upgrades, so the faster you make that money, the quicker you can expand your businesses.

2 **USE UPGRADES WISELY**
Always buy the cheapest available upgrades. Doing this, you will be able to buy several at a time, rather than one big upgrade. Try to focus on the ones that make the most money early on.

3 **GO CRAZY WITH YOUR BUILDING**
You're making all that money, so spend it how you like! If you want to paint everything pink, then do it. Why not? Unless the tycoon asks you to stick to a theme, just have fun and express yourself.

4 **PLAY WITH FRIENDS**
You can play a lot of tycoon games with friends. Not always in the same business or building, but running two companies next door to each other makes it more of a fun competition.

5 **PLAY EVERY DAY**
It's often worth checking in on your tycoon games every day, even if you only play for a few minutes. This is because a lot of them will offer rewards for playing. That extra money always helps!

ROBLOX TRIVIA

Did you know that Roblox is one of the most popular platforms on the planet? We could say that it's the most popular in the universe, but we're unsure if aliens have found a better game! With Roblox played by so many people, it's amazing just what it has achieved.

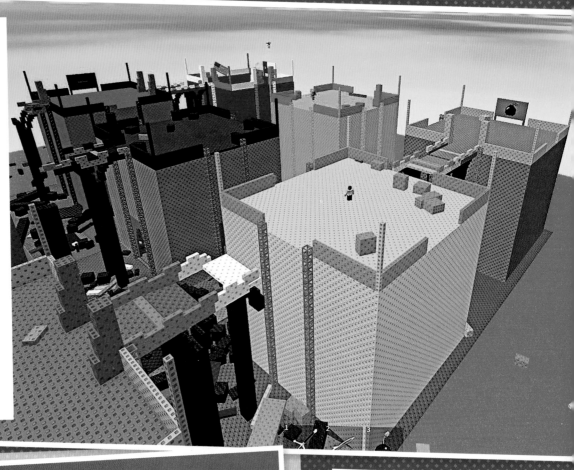

Roblox first launched in September 2006

That's 17 years ago! The first playable game was called Rocket Arena and it had players battling each other on bridges above a lake of lava. To win, you needed to destroy the other team's bridges using jets and rockets. Unfortunately, the game is unplayable nowadays due to the updates Roblox has gone through over the years.

Before the game was called Roblox, it was known as DynaBlocks. Which name do you prefer? It was created by two people, David Baszucki and Erik Cassel.

The ten most popular games last year:

1. Murder Mystery 2
2. Shindo Life
3. Meep City
4. Blox Fruits
5. Brookhaven RP
6. Adopt Me!
7. Pet Simulator X
8. Sonic Speed Simulator
9. King Legacy
10. Mining Simulator 2

The pet simulator game, Adopt Me! is the most popular game of all time. As of October 2022 the game had reached 30.5 billion visits. That's more visits than there are people on Earth. In October 2019 Adopt Me! was so popular it crashed Roblox. Not just their servers, but the entire game! Nothing would run until Roblox engineers could fix the problem.

There are over 40 million different games on the Roblox platform!

It can take as little as one month to create a game with Roblox Studio if you set aside enough hours per day. The studio software is very easy to use and allows anyone to create a game, whether young or old. What are you waiting for?

Roblox has played host to lots of concerts and experiences, seeing big celebrities perform or launch new projects. Did you catch Lil Nas X or George Ezra in concert? Did you visit the Grammy music awards? Or the BRITs VIP party? Even huge companies like NIKE and Nickelodeon are creating in-game experiences for you to explore. We can't wait to see what comes next!

Roblox has a university. Kind of. It's a place for players to learn how to program games for Roblox. The university has a whole library of YouTube videos for people to learn the basics, all the way up to the more difficult tasks.

ROLE-PLAYING GAMES

Role-playing games are some of the most popular on Roblox. There's something wonderful about being able to step into the shoes of someone else. You can do anything or live anywhere. Perhaps you want to experience a world unlike ours, or be a superhero, or maybe you just want to drive!

TAXI BOSS

Taxi Boss is a driving game where your only role is to drive a taxi through the city. That's it. It's quite a simple idea really, but it's one of those games where you just want to play one more game. Or, in this case, pick up one more passenger.

After choosing your starter car, you're let loose in the city. You cruise around looking for customers standing on the side of the road. Each one has a star rating above their head telling you how difficult their route might be, or whether your taxi service is good enough to pick them up. At first you'll drive short routes, but they'll be more challenging before long.

Of course, each passenger pays their way and soon you'll have a nice amount of in-game cash in the bank, ready for a car upgrade. Faster cars mean dropping your passengers off quicker and doing more jobs to earn more money. Because each ride doesn't take too long, it's easy to just keep playing and driving. You'll soon find yourself saying 'This is my last passenger' and when you drop them off, you'll see another close by and say 'Oh, alright, one more then'.

ADOPT ME!

It's hard to think that Adopt Me! is a role-playing game, when so many people play to collect the pets. There are so many things to do in the game, but of course, the pets are why everyone starts playing Adopt Me! They're all so cute and the seasonal pets get everyone excited. It's brilliant for collectors, and being able to combine extra pets to make them rarer makes it even more fun!

You have a house to decorate, cars to drive around and mini games to play. When you're not hatching new pets, the world is yours to explore. You can really live out a new role, by pretending to be someone different. You might want to live in a large house surrounded by all your pets; or perhaps you want to buy a nice car and tour around the neighbourhoods giving rides to other people.

You can even play as a baby and have everyone else take care of you! When you first play Adopt Me! you can choose to be a baby or an adult. If you choose baby, your life will be a little easier. You and your friends can become a little family who have lovely days out or stay at home playing with their pets. It's all your choice, so get going.

WELCOME TO BLOXBURG

Welcome to Bloxburg is one of the biggest names in Roblox. It has always been popular, not just in the role-play category, but across all of Roblox. In fact, since its release in 2016, the game has had over five billion visits. This is the only game we feature in this book that costs Robux to play, simply because it's so good. It costs 25 Robux to join, but if you can afford it, this game is worth every penny.

Everything revolves around the city of Bloxburg. You can build a house, go shopping, get a job and earn money. This is a full-on life experience. You have to really invest in your digital life to get the most from the game. It doesn't take long to feel at home in Bloxburg.

Once you've picked a place to build your home and you've found a great job (there are over 12 jobs to choose from) you need to take care of your avatar. Keep them fed, make them happy and be sure they're living their best life. It's kind of like treating them how you would want to be treated. You want a fun job, a nice house, a good car and plenty of friends. Oh, did we mention you can do all of this with your friends and family? They can even move in next door.

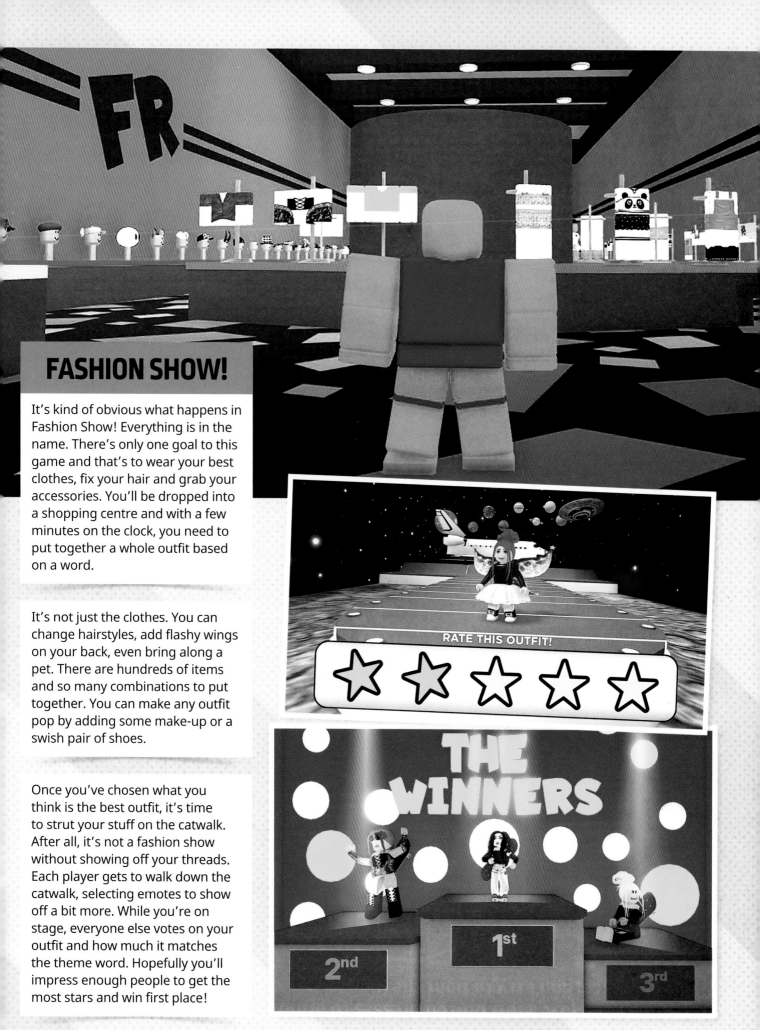

FASHION SHOW!

It's kind of obvious what happens in Fashion Show! Everything is in the name. There's only one goal to this game and that's to wear your best clothes, fix your hair and grab your accessories. You'll be dropped into a shopping centre and with a few minutes on the clock, you need to put together a whole outfit based on a word.

It's not just the clothes. You can change hairstyles, add flashy wings on your back, even bring along a pet. There are hundreds of items and so many combinations to put together. You can make any outfit pop by adding some make-up or a swish pair of shoes.

Once you've chosen what you think is the best outfit, it's time to strut your stuff on the catwalk. After all, it's not a fashion show without showing off your threads. Each player gets to walk down the catwalk, selecting emotes to show off a bit more. While you're on stage, everyone else votes on your outfit and how much it matches the theme word. Hopefully you'll impress enough people to get the most stars and win first place!

RATE THIS OUTFIT!

THE WINNERS

2nd

1st

3rd

35

BROOKHAVEN RP

If you want a proper role-playing experience, then Brookhaven might be the place to visit. It has everything you need to choose a role and live it freely. There are shops to visit, an arcade, a cinema, some coffee shops, a diner, an airport ... it feels like the list goes on and on. So much!

Then you have your house and car, which let you have house guests and a way to get around the huge town. It's best to think of Brookhaven as a complete online life – somewhere to get together with others and really be who you want to be. You can choose a new name, have one of many different jobs and decorate a beautiful house. Lots of role-play games offer these experiences, but here you can even choose how to animate your avatar. You can dance in the local disco, do backflips in the gym or laugh when someone tells a funny joke.

Brookhaven offers you so many things to do, that you don't even have to play with other people. It can become a safe place for you to be who you want to be, or who you feel you really are. Then again, you can invite your real friends and set up a little group where you all live differently from your real lives, but you can still hang out, play games and laugh together.

ROLE-PLAYING GAMES
FIVE TOP TIPS

1 BE CAREFUL
Role-playing often needs other people to join you, so you can live a new role online. Sometimes other players can be mean, but just ignore anyone who is being rude. When playing these games, try to play with people you know in you everyday life, so you can really enjoy the fun together.

2 BE KIND
Treat others with kindness and try to understand why they're playing this game in the first place. Most want to have fun or keep in touch with friends through playing. Treat others how you would want to be treated, to help make sure everyone has a good time.

3 BE CREATIVE
This isn't just about decorating your house, but also about what role you might want to play. It's fun to be a famous rock star who lives in a fancy house, but what about being a clown or an astronaut? You could be an adventurer just hanging out around town in between epic life-threatening expeditions!

4 GET TO KNOW THE TOWN
Exploring the large towns and social areas in these games can be a big part of the fun. Finding new buildings to hang out in or a great stretch of road to race cars on can feel really satisfying. You can then tell others, or keep it as a secret place to chill.

5 HAVE FUN!
Above all, these games are created for you to have fun. Whether you're selling ice cream in the local shop, wearing wacky clothes on the catwalk or zooming around the city streets, you're playing because it makes you happy. Remember to have fun when trying out new games and roles.

THOSE ARE FIGHTING WORDS!

BAM!

Whether it's a clicker, a simulator or a tower defence, there are plenty of ways to fight or battle. You don't need to have all the skills, as a lot of these games need just a few button presses to bring the brawls. Just one piece of advice: don't try to fight the biggest opponent without practice!

BLOX FRUITS

Blox Fruits is a bit like an MMORPG. That might seem like a bunch of random letters, but it means "Massively Multiplayer Online Role-Playing Game". It's a game where lots of people exist in one world and they fight, talk and explore together. You have to upgrade your character by fighting enemies and completing quests. You can do these alone or with others.

As you grow, you'll be able to take on harder challenges and fight bigger bosses. You'll soon need to buy more fruits, which will give your character unique abilities.

BOOM!

SLAP BATTLES

The name of this game kind of says it all. It's quite simple, you're dropped into a small arena with a bunch of other players and you have to eliminate each other by slapping. You can just run up to another player and slap them. This sends them spinning into the air and you score a slap point. Thankfully, respawns are really fast, so the action never stops.

There are also special abilities available, such as fart power, which gives you a quick burst of speed, or snow glove, which freezes opponents and slows them down.

ANIME TYCOON

This fighter starts out like a regular tycoon game. You get a base and slowly earn money, allowing you to walk over buttons that will upgrade your home area. You can buy droppers, which give extra cash, as well as creating the building itself. The best bit? There are gear pods to purchase which give you amazing fighting moves from your favourite anime styles.

These powerful moves are used outside your base, where you'll find other players wandering around. You can walk up to anyone and begin fighting, using each fancy move to try to beat them before they can eliminate you. Don't worry if you get beaten, you'll spawn back in your area; you might just need to save up extra cash for stronger fighting skills. Soon you'll be earning millions while bashing!

ZAP!

POW!

ALL STAR TOWER DEFENSE

Tower defence games have been popular for many years now. You'll find yourself stood on a battlefield, with monsters invading along a path at one end. It's your job to place characters and weapons next to the path in order to fight the baddies. Every once in a while, a boss will being trudging down that path, so you'll need to be prepared and make sure you have the best fighters on the field and that they're upgraded.

Think about where everyone should go. If you have a fighter who shoots from a distance, make sure they're covering the path from far away, then they can't get attacked. If you've got some big bruisers who fight up-close, maybe have those lining the path right at the start to weaken the enemy.

FIVE OF THE BEST
VEHICLE GAMES

Sometimes the most fun you can have in video games is jumping into a fast car and tearing around some city streets. Of course, vehicles come in all shapes and sizes. It's not just cars you can use in Roblox, but also skateboards, boats, planes, fire trucks and more.

DRIVING EMPIRE

Let's start our vehicle section with a gorgeous racing game where each car looks like it just rolled out of a showroom. Of course, you start out with a pretty basic car, but even the basic cars in Driving Empire are stunning to look at and drive.

This is definitely more realistic than other racing games on Roblox. There are buttons for everything! You can switch your gears from automatic to manual, control the radio and headlights, even slam on the emergency brake for some skids and drifting. But it's also fun to just cruise the city streets, which will slowly earn you more money to use in the game.

You can also earn money by choosing a role, which means either becoming a criminal or a member of the police force. This gives you much more to do in the game and can provide you with loads of entertaining experiences to make your driving more fun.

CAR CRUSHERS 2

This game definitely does what it says in the title. You spawn a car, drive it into a special room and the car gets destroyed. It's a lot of fun watching the cars crumble into pieces. The bodywork pops off, the engine falls apart, and sometimes it all catches fire. Destruction, within a game is great ... just don't do it outside of such games!

It's not just cars you can destroy in Car Crushers 2. You can choose vans, trucks and loads more vehicles. Then, if you're not feeling the crushing, you can have the vehicle attacked with lasers, or dropped into a large blender. You can even freeze it and watch as it smashes into icy sections, or you can burn it with a fire hotter than dragon's breath.

Anything goes really. Sometimes the simple methods are the best; like driving the car down some stairs and watching it flip end-over-end until it shatters. Why are we smashing these cars? Well, firstly because it's fun, but more importantly, because you earn points for great smashes. These points then unlock more cars and even more ways to destroy them.

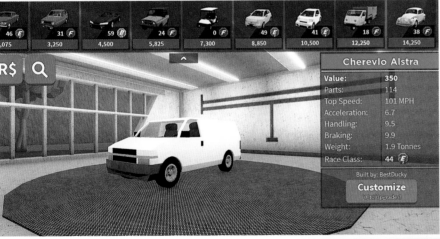

46 ⒠	31 ⒡	59 ⒤	24 ⒡	0 ⒡	49 ⒤	41 ⒠	18 ⒡	38 ⒡
2,075	3,250	4,500	5,825	7,300	8,850	10,500	12,250	14,250

Cherevlo Alstra

Value:	350
Parts:	114
Top Speed:	101 MPH
Acceleration:	6.7
Handling:	9.5
Braking:	9.9
Weight:	1.9 Tonnes
Race Class:	44 ⒠

Built by: BestDucky

Customize
[0/12 Upgrades]

EMERGENCY RESPONSE: LIBERTY COUNTY

In Liberty County, life is about more than vehicles. It's about the job you do. You can choose from several jobs, all of them in emergency response, from policing to firefighting. This is very much a role-play game where much of your time will be spent driving vehicles.

If you choose to fight crime, it's your job to patrol areas, stop criminals from committing crimes and lock them up. If you choose to fight fires, then you can help with emergency situations. For those wanting to drive around with the siren blaring, you can definitely do that. But, for those who want more depth to their gaming, you can do much more than zooming around.

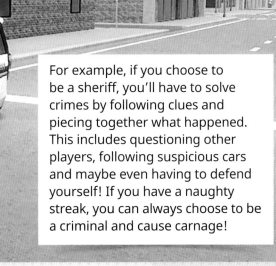

For example, if you choose to be a sheriff, you'll have to solve crimes by following clues and piecing together what happened. This includes questioning other players, following suspicious cars and maybe even having to defend yourself! If you have a naughty streak, you can always choose to be a criminal and cause carnage!

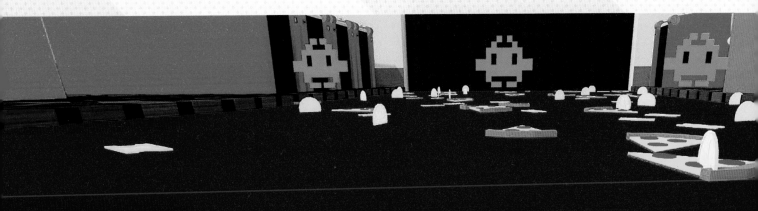

BUILD A BOAT FOR TREASURE

Have you ever wanted to be a pirate? Or a sailor? Pirate sounds more exciting to us. If you want to be a pirate and search for treasure, you're going to need a boat. To build a boat, you get a selection of blocks and items. In your small starting area, you need to build the best boat you can with the limited materials you have available.

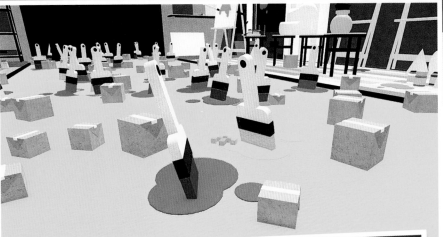

You might only have eight blocks and an engine, so end up creating more of a raft. Then it's time to launch your boat into the water, where you'll have to survive as long as possible. There's a long stretch of water between you and the mega treasures, and in that water are rocks and obstacles. If you bump into any of these, your boat will begin to fall apart.

Thankfully, instead of drowning, you end up back in your starting area with a few more building materials – and the chance to get even more. This means a better boat! Eventually, you'll be spending more time building than sailing, but you can craft some incredible vessels. Will yours make it safely across to the treasure?

SPLASH

Skateboarding has always been cool. It's a brilliant sport that makes people feel like they can fly through the air. In the offline world, it takes a lot of practice just to stay up straight on a skateboard. Thankfully, Roblox has a skating game that lets you feel like a pro.

It's really quite easy to start skateboarding and performing tricks. You only need a few buttons; jump, grab and flip. Each is probably quite obvious, but just in case, these buttons allow you to jump with the board attached to your feet. You can also do fancy grabs when using the grab button and holding a direction key. Lastly, you can flip the board and perform kick flips and other tricks with wicked names.

Just make sure you don't fly off the ramps and into other players. Or, like us, spin the board and your body for too long and faceplant straight into the ramp!

FIVE TOP TIPS

1 LEARN
This one is for the racers. If you have a course you need to complete, don't worry about finishing first right away. Take some time to learn the course. This will help you prepare for difficult corners and any obstacles.

2 CORNERS
To get the best times in a race and win, you need to learn how to drive around corners. The idea is to drive into the corner slowly and come out of it quickly. This means braking a little as you approach, taking the turn, and accelerating out of the corner.

3 SHOP FIRST, SPEND LATER
When you start any game with vehicles, make sure to check out the shop right away and decide on a car that you want. Then you'll know how much money you need to earn before heading back to the store to buy it later.

4 CHECK THE STATS
Some driving games are really detailed, featuring loads of stats. These normally show you how fast the car can go, whether it corners well and how quickly it can drive along a straight road. Learn what these mean and how they apply to the car you want to buy. You don't want to just buy the pretty cars if you want to win races.

5 BUT YOU CAN GO SLOW
You don't have to buy the fastest cars (although they're really good fun!) you could just buy a really slick car and take your time cruising around, looking at the streets. And remember, Roblox can take screenshots of the game, so park up somewhere nice and take some photos of your car.

FOR THE LOVE OF PETS

We love Roblox pets so much, we needed a second section dedicated to them! You really can get pets in a lot of games nowadays, even games where all you do is jump for long distances. But we don't mind, it just means we can hatch more eggs and see more adorable little faces.

MEEPCITY

Are meeps actually pets? They definitely feel like pets. They're all tiny and colourful and cute! Meep City is such a popular game and the meeps come with you to play mini games and meet your friends! It makes us sad that meeps aren't available in real life. Imagine taking a meep with you to school, or work. They could sit under your desk and brighten up your day!

COLLECT ALL PETS

This game just has the perfect title, doesn't it?! That's exactly what we all want to do. This cute pet collector is so lovely to look at. The pets are all round and sweet, but then we fuse five pets together to get these cubed creatures and we fall in love all over again! Pet fusion is so much fun, because you never know what you'll get in the end! Will you get something sweet and lovely, or will you breed something a bit monstrous?

FIVE OF THE GREATEST
ACTION GAMES

Roblox is a great place to come if you want all-out action games that will have you grinning from ear to ear. Whether you want role-playing games, shooters or team games, there's something for everyone. If you want some action ... just have a look at these.

BE A PARKOUR NINJA

We didn't even know that a 'parkour ninja' was a thing until we stumbled across this game. Really, any ninja is a parkour ninja if they do a lot of climbing and jumping around. It's kind of maxed-out here though. These ninjas can do double jumps, wall-jump up tall structures and even dash through the air. All so that they can attack enemy players. Talk about mad skills.

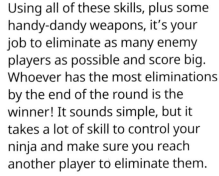

Using all of these skills, plus some handy-dandy weapons, it's your job to eliminate as many enemy players as possible and score big. Whoever has the most eliminations by the end of the round is the winner! It sounds simple, but it takes a lot of skill to control your ninja and make sure you reach another player to eliminate them.

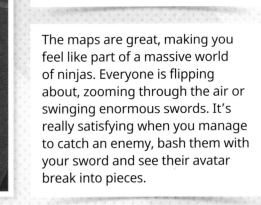

The maps are great, making you feel like part of a massive world of ninjas. Everyone is flipping about, zooming through the air or swinging enormous swords. It's really satisfying when you manage to catch an enemy, bash them with your sword and see their avatar break into pieces.

BIG PAINTBALL

If you want a big, bright and colourful shooting game, then Big Paintball is the game for you. Shooting games can come in various forms. Sometimes they're hyper-realistic, based on weapons from real life. Other times they can be a bit wacky and imaginative. Big Paintball is definitely one of the wackier ones. It's so much fun!

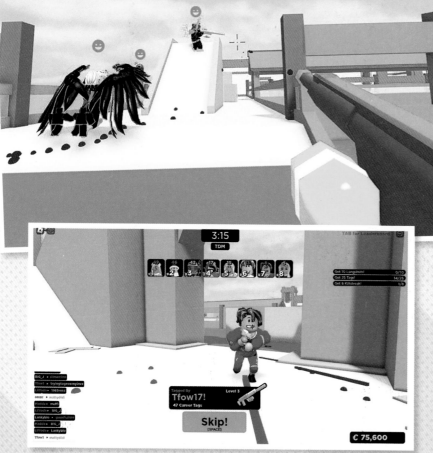

As the name suggests, you'll be firing paintballs at each other. You can fight on a team, or play on your own. As you hit other players and eliminate them, you'll earn credits which can be spent on unlocking new weapons. The more players you hit, the more credits you'll earn, but also you'll be rewarded with abilities to help you eliminate even more people.

For example, you can unlock a radar which shows you where other players are hiding. Or a sentry turret, which places a gun that fires at players automatically. There's even a drone you can control! And this all happens in a game with big splotches of colourful paint being blasted at each other, much like real-life paintball ... without the mess to clean up afterwards!

NINJA LEGENDS

One glance at Roblox and you would think everyone wants to be a ninja! There are so many great games about becoming a martial arts and weapons expert who dashes around in cool clothes. Actually, that does sound pretty awesome – we'd like to be ninjas too! Thankfully, we have Ninja Legends, which is a fighting game in which you need to train and battle in order to become the best ninja in the whole game.

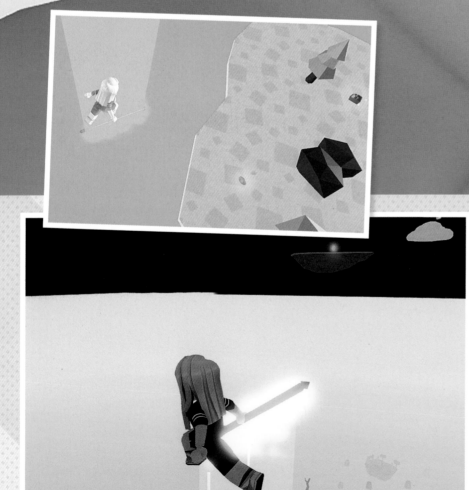

You can unlock weapons and special powers across different islands, collect pets to help you kick butt and that's all before you meet some of the game's huge and terrifying bosses. Seriously, they're massive and they make you feel like you'll never win. But if you put in work in the dojo, you'll be ready to take on even the biggest monsters in the game.

This is the closest you might get to being an action movie star. Make sure you put in the work, train up those skills and be ready for a fight! The more you brawl, the more your ninja will level-up and quickly turn into a legend.

PHANTOM FORCES

If you're accurate with your aim and get a rush from hectic shootouts, then Phantom Forces should definitely be on your Roblox list! It can be a complex and challenging game, but get to grips with it and this first-person shooter is one of the very best in the genre. Load up and roll out ...

Phantom Forces sees two teams – the blue-tagged Phantoms and the orange Ghosts – face off around a series of maps. There are different game modes, a huge selection of weapons, loadouts and team tactics to master. You need to go all in for this mission!

In your primary loadout slot will be machines such as snipers and assault rifles, which are essential for long- and mid-range duels. These often have a high accuracy and will be automatic or semi-automatic firing, which means they can fire at a faster rate!

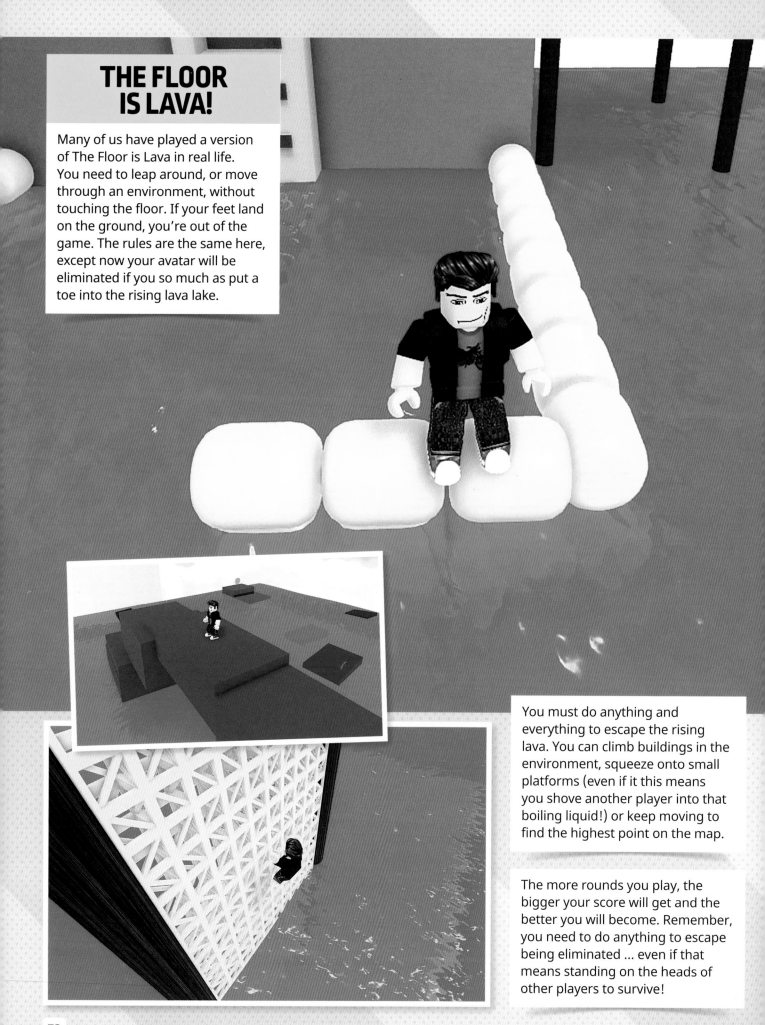

THE FLOOR IS LAVA!

Many of us have played a version of The Floor is Lava in real life. You need to leap around, or move through an environment, without touching the floor. If your feet land on the ground, you're out of the game. The rules are the same here, except now your avatar will be eliminated if you so much as put a toe into the rising lava lake.

You must do anything and everything to escape the rising lava. You can climb buildings in the environment, squeeze onto small platforms (even if it this means you shove another player into that boiling liquid!) or keep moving to find the highest point on the map.

The more rounds you play, the bigger your score will get and the better you will become. Remember, you need to do anything to escape being eliminated ... even if that means standing on the heads of other players to survive!

FIVE TOP TIPS

1 PRACTISE!
If you want to be great at any game, not just action games, you need to practise and put in plenty of time building your skills. Not only will this make you a better player, but you'll feel more confident in your playing.

2 GRAB SOME FRIENDS
While many of these action games can be played alone, they can be more fun with some buddies. Send your friends some invites, set yourselves challenges and work together to be the best team around.

3 DON'T TAKE THE GAMES TOO SERIOUSLY
These are just games. Taking games too seriously can mean getting angry or upset when things don't go your way. You can be competitive without it making you feel sad if you lose a game. Just enjoy playing with others and celebrate your wins. If you lose, just load up the game again and try once more.

4 WIRED VS WIRELESS
A good tip for any online games, really. Try to have your console or PC connected to the internet via a cable, rather than wireless. This will allow you to have a better connection and react faster to what's happening on the screen than some of your opponents.

5 LOOK FOR TIPS
There are a lot of YouTube videos and websites that offer great tips on how to get better at lots of games. Most times they will offer advice on the best weapons or the most useful skills to focus on, making you a better player.

BREAKING APART

Roblox has always had great physics, so your avatar's arms and legs wave around naturally when it's launched into the air. The same goes for when your avatar has an accident with an enemy and falls to pieces. Just remember not to try these at home. You aren't a Roblox avatar!

BROKEN BONES IV

The goal in Broken Bones IV is simple: just give your avatar a rough ride! Starting at the top of a cliff, you can jump over the edge and watch as your avatar flails its arms and legs, plummeting towards the bottom. Of course, once you land, it's with a few bumps and bruises, and you're awarded points for each break. It's often very funny watching the carnage because it's just completely over the top!

As you progress through the game and score more points, you can unlock exciting new locations in which to damage your poor avatar. It never gets old!

THE DROPPER

Dropper games have been popular for a few years now. Because of how simple they are, everyone can play. Your avatar starts on the edge of a hole – well, it's more of a long tunnel. You have to jump in and fall all the way to safety at the bottom. Trust us, there's a soft landing at the end. Take your time, navigate well and just enjoy the thrill of falling. Oh, did we mention the tunnel is filled with dangers that destroy your avatar with one touch?

Thankfully, you can guide your avatar as it falls. You'll need to navigate objects large and small, and as the levels get tougher, you'll be diving through smaller gaps too. Other players can also fall at the same time as you, which makes for hilarious competition.

RAGDOLL SIMULATOR

Ragdoll Simulator is a giant (dangerous) playground. It's designed with damage in mind. As soon as you spawn, you will realise your avatar won't survive what lies ahead. There's a hammer that squashes you, a cannon that fires you into the air, slides and rollercoasters that slam you into pieces. There are even modes dedicated to making the avatar collapse into pieces and then be carried along at high speed. Usually all of these death traps will end in a satisfying splat or crumbling apart of arms and legs, which can't be avoided. Try to enjoy the hilarious journey and not worry about your avatar – there's nothing you can do for them ... except watch and laugh!

FIVE GREAT
PvP GAMES

A large portion of the games on Roblox are designed to be played against others. These are known as PvP (player vs player) games. PvP can appear within lots of categories and have you playing as part of a team or running solo. If you're here to play competitively, you MUST try out these!

BED WARS

Can you protect your precious bed no matter what? Because there are players trying to destroy it and you must do everything in your power to stop this from happening. It sounds like a bonkers game, and it is, to be honest.

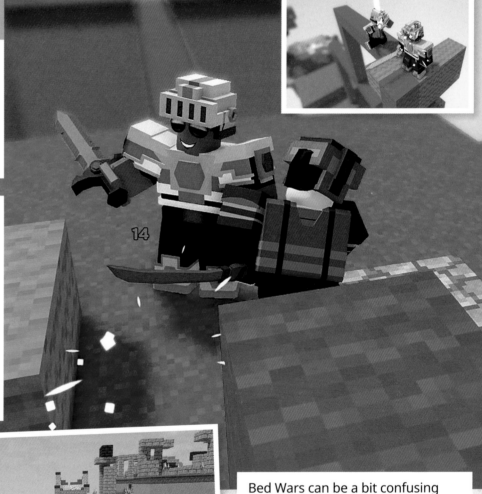

Players aren't only trying to destroy your bed, they're also trying to destroy you. Because without a line of defence, it makes the bed breaking a lot easier. Oh, and if they do break your bed, it means you can no longer respawn, leaving you with just one life. When you aren't fighting, you'll be both exploring and defending. This is done with different types of blocks you can buy in-game.

Bed Wars can be a bit confusing for new players. Thankfully, the game can be a little easier to play if you choose the right kits. Kits are kind of like character classes, and each one has its own abilities. Some may come with more health, making them harder to eliminate, while another may be able to break blocks faster. Just keep in mind three goals; fight, defend your bed, explore ... and always have fun.

COMBAT WARRIORS

Combat Warriors is an epic fighting game where you're dropped onto a map with a set of items and weapons, and must survive, while eliminating other players. The starting items of a baton, some throwable weapons and a bear trap will do quite nicely for a while. After some time though, you'll want to spend some points on bigger and better weapons.

The maps you'll fight on are really exciting and varied, with lots of places to hide when you need to heal, or to launch surprise attacks on your opponents. Each game feels fast and crazy, as the rounds only last a few minutes and you need to score as many eliminations as possible in that time.

While you can play this with friends, you will end up having to fight each other, so prepare yourself for all-out war and don't fall out over it!

MURDER MYSTERY 2

Everyone loves a mystery to solve. Or to be a part of the mystery. In this game, the goal changes depending on who you play as. When everyone joins the game, they're given a role they have to act out. There are 12 players: 1 murderer, 1 sheriff and 10 other innocent individuals.

If you start as the sheriff, you need to protect the innocent people by using your gun. The murderer spawns with a weapon and must eliminate all the innocents and the sheriff before time runs out, to win the game. If the sheriff is eliminated, they drop their gun and an innocent can collect it to become the new sheriff.

If you're not a murderer or sheriff, you simply need to stay alive by hiding, running or staying close to the other innocents ... but can you trust them and work out who the murderer is before they get you? Will you all work together or will you try to survive on your own? Whatever you choose, you need to stay alive and make sure the killer is captured, before it's too late!

FLAG WARS

Flag Wars is based on a very popular PvP mode that has appeared in video games for over 20 years. Capture the flag often features in pretty much all multiplayer games. The goal is to steal your opponent's flag from their base and carry it back to yours. If you get eliminated, you will drop the flag. If none of your teammates collect it, then it will vanish and go back to your opponent's base.

While you're trying your hardest to steal their flag, they will be doing the same. They want your flag, because whoever steals the most flags will win the game. So you have a choice to make, do you go on the attack and try to steal their flag, or do you play defensively and stay in your base to watch over your team flag?

Sometimes it's worth doing a bit of both, depending on where you spawn or what weapon you have available. If you have a long-range rifle, for example, then you can watch over your flag from a distance while slowly edging closer to the enemy flag. However you play, Flag Wars is a great experience for players looking for fun ways to play as a team.

ELIMINATION TOWER

If you've ever wanted to appear on a television game show, then Elimination Tower is for you! Your avatar finds itself thrown into a game show with a bunch of other players. You need to win mini-games, which then give you the chance to choose players to eliminate. So, if you win the first game, you'll pick four players who go into an elimination game.

Bruce Dapples
Each round everyone will participate in a challenge...

As each round passes, fewer and fewer players will move forward. The best of the best will still be standing at the end and the nerves might kick in as you play to win.

Of course, there's a chance that you'll lose the game and be chosen to fight against your own elimination. Either way, you'll be playing a lot of mini-games that test your skills in a number of ways, such as snowball throwing and stunt courses. It's great to play with a group of friends and watch as they have to take their turns!

FIVE TOP TIPS

1 PLAY TO YOUR STRENGTH

You might find yourself in a shooting game, and perhaps you're great at sniping from a distance. If that's the case, then get out there fast and grab that sniper rifle. Maybe you're great at obby games, in which case seek out PvP games focused on parkour.

2 BE A TEAM PLAYER

A lot of the PvP games on Roblox are team-based. If you find yourself on a team, then communicate and work together. A team will only win if everyone is playing together. You don't even need a microphone, you can type in the chat box to discuss tactics with your team.

3 PRACTISE!

We could write this on all of our tips pages, but it's most important in PvP. You won't score as many wins if you don't play often and learn about maps or abilities. You don't have to be playing every minute of the day, but if you want to be good, then focus your Roblox time on your favourite PvP game.

4 DO YOUR BEST

This is all you can ever do. Nobody is asking for more than your best. As long as you're trying and learning, then you are doing the best you can and that means you're having fun.

5 JUST HAVE FUN

Speaking of having fun, this is why we play games. We don't play to get angry or upset when we lose or when something goes wrong. We start playing because we want to have a good time. If you focus on having fun, then each game will be a great experience.

SIMULATOR GAMES

Roblox is filled with oddball games, Most of which are found in the simulator category. There are animal simulators, business simulators, even wizard simulators. With so many to play, we've pulled together some of the more unique simulator games!

MERGE SIMULATOR

Merge Simulator is a game about waiting. For a while at least. The idea is simple, blocks with numbers on will appear in your little arena and you must match the numbers. However, when the blocks are merged, they add together to produce a new – higher – number. These must then be merged together, again and again to reach ridiculously high numbers.

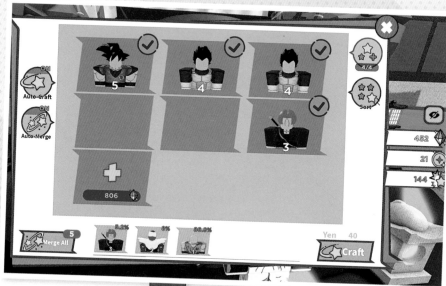

There's a fair amount of waiting at first, because the blocks take a while to appear, but moving them around is pretty quick. Thankfully, matching the blocks rewards coins and these coins can be spent to make sure the blocks spawn faster, or even start at a higher number to save the amount of merging you'll need to do.

It's quite satisfying watching the blocks join and pop out a new cube. This ends up being an odd crossover of maths game and simulator. Remember when we said that simulators can be about anything? We bet you didn't think about colourful number blocks!

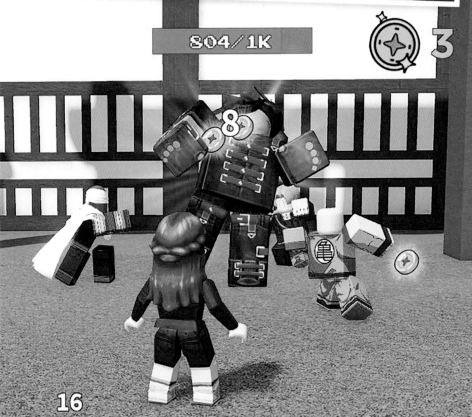

16

WEAPON FIGHTING SIMULATOR

There are SO MANY fighting simulators or training simulators. Most of them require some clicking or pressing of buttons in order to get stronger. There's a little of that here, but it feels a bit more exciting. The first stop is buying an egg. Not a pet this time though, this egg will hatch your first weapon. Probably a sword. You use this weapon (which flies around your body) to destroy items, which drop gold and experience (XP) gems.

Collecting these drops will allow you to buy better weapons from the egg shop, but also level-up the weapons you already have. You'll be destroying the items quite happily, but if you look closely, there's a new area in the distance with a padlock. Suddenly, you want to explore beyond the gate. Not so fast!

In order to open this padlock and explore further, you need to defeat a boss monster. You'll soon find yourself in a small arena with a large creature trying to gobble you up. It's up to your weapons to defeat this creature, all while you try to stay clear of it. Thankfully, you'll get some magic spells too, but if you haven't put in the work to level-up, you'll find yourself flattened and need to get back to your training before you can fight and win. Trust us, what's behind that gate is worth it.

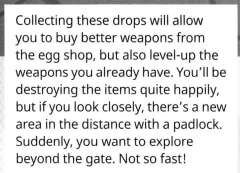

Diamond Pile
1.98K

63

SMASHING SIMULATOR X

There's something wonderful about smashing things. Not in real life, obviously! That would get us in trouble. In video games, smashing and destroying is often a big part of what happens. With this Roblox game, it's the ONLY thing that happens. Smashing Simulator X asks you to smash everything in sight. First using objects such as pillows and eventually working up to huge weights.

Starting in the office district, you break down trees, signs and park benches. Each object you break earns you some gold coins, which can be used to buy new weapons that smash with more power than ever. You can also buy some pets, which help add more damage to your weapon.

Slowly, as your power increases and you earn more money, you can unlock new areas with more objects to smash. And the smashing is so much fun! Everything explodes into small pieces with a satisfying crash sound. You can smash up a playground, a building crane, an airport lounge, and all of them crumble brilliantly.

MINION SIMULATOR

This simulator is very much about the little minions who help you along the way, but it's also a bit of a mining simulator as you'll be doing a lot of digging. So many Roblox games feature pets hatching from eggs nowadays. For this sim, it's the most important thing to do. Starting with very basic minions hatched from the earliest eggs, you'll be breaking down piles of gold and gems, which are collected to upgrade tools and buy new minion eggs.

The better the minions you have with you, the faster you'll be able to break down these piles of materials. Rare and ultra-rare pets are the best, but can be hard to find. Thankfully, all it means is a bit more mining and digging to earn some more in-game cash.

It doesn't take long to start breaking down piles worth millions of gems, then it's time to move on to a new zone, with new pets and new challenges. Of course, there's also a leaderboard to show how well you're doing compared to other players – it's always great to see your name up there after some new upgrades.

MINING SIMULATOR 2

Okay, this one is actually about mining. There's a pickaxe and you'll be digging out materials such as iron, gold and fossils. As with other sim games, Mining Simulator 2 is all about getting the highest score you can. The score is in-game money and the money is earned by digging out those precious materials and selling them at the local shop.

You'll start off equipped with a tiny backpack and a weak pickaxe. Unfortunately, your backpack will fill up fast with minerals and dirt, meaning often travelling back to the surface to sell them both. Getting a bigger backpack keeps you digging for longer, but so does having a stronger tool, which you can buy with your earnings.

Perhaps the best bit of Mining Simulator 2 is working with or against other players. Everyone is digging in the same mineshaft, which goes down for miles. You may be digging away and suddenly find yourself in a huge cave that someone else has mined. Or you may plummet long distances from an unexpected drop (don't worry, there's no fall damage) from someone tunnelling straight down. Just keep digging and selling, and eventually you'll be speeding through the layers of dirt, stone, ice and more!

FIVE TOP TIPS

1 PETS

Most of these simulators, and plenty of others, will feature pets. This isn't just because pets are cute and feature in most games now, but because they make you more powerful or they allow you to collect more materials.

2 MAKE MONEY FAST

You're going to want to upgrade your starting area or tool very quickly as it will make earning in-game money a lot faster. Choose the upgrades that will allow you to earn more.

3 TRY THEM OUT

Not all simulators offer the same experience, even if they share the name 'simulator'. Most of them play very differently to each other. Some will have you pressing buttons on the floor, some can have you moving things around, while others might have nearby players attacking you!

4 PLAY TOGETHER

Some simulator games allow you and a friend to play together, in charge of your own sections of the simulator. It can be really fun watching your friend rushing around next to you.

5 TAKE BREAKS

Simulators, or any other game where you're chasing a high score, can get quite addictive. Make sure to take breaks regularly. It doesn't matter if another player overtakes your score. You'll get there again.

67

LET'S GET SPORTY

Here are some fun sporting games to play inside, but remember to get out every so often and get some fresh air, take a break from your games and hang out with friends. Playing games outside is just as fun as playing games on Roblox. In fact, all games rule!

SHOCKWAVE RACING

Okay, so this is just running, right? Nope. This is running as if you were the fastest person alive, in an action film trying to escape from bad guys. Nothing beats leaping over gaps, dodging around moving platforms and running across walls. It's like running while your butt is on fire, just speeding through each area in search of water. This really is one of the fastest games we've ever played!

TPS: STREET SOCCER

If football (also known as soccer) is your thing, but you don't want to get all sweaty while playing, then play online instead. It's kind of like football in real life, but stripped down to the most important aspects. All the skills are needed, but the ball can't go out of bounds and there are only a few players on each team. It makes everything much more chaotic and crazy. Grab your friends and have a kickabout of carnage!

FLY RACE

Fly Race is a very simple game. It's so simple, even your granny could play it. All you need to do is run up a ramp, which blasts you into the distance. As you land, you'll be rewarded with studs. You can use your studs like coins and buy pets, that will help you jump farther. Each jump also upgrades your avatar a little, meaning every new jump will be a personal high score.

Where Fly Race gets interesting is when you compete against other players. Sometimes there will be someone who is neck-and-neck with your jumps. And all you want to do is beat them. Of course, pets will help, but there are also little rocket items scattered across the floor, which will each give a small boost to your leap. Time for lift off!

STAYING SAFE ONLINE

YOUNGER FANS' GUIDE

Spending time online is great fun. These games might be your first experience of digital socialising, so here are a few simple rules to help you stay safe and keep the internet an awesome place to spend time:

• Never give out your real name – don't use it as your username.
• Never give out any of your personal details.
• Never tell anybody which school you go to or how old you are.
• Never tell anybody your password, except a parent or guardian.
• Before registering for any account, ask a parent or guardian for permission.
• Take regular breaks, as well as playing with parents nearby, or in shared family rooms.
• Always tell a parent or guardian if something is worrying you.

PARENTS' GUIDE

ONLINE CHAT
In most games, there is live on-screen text chat between users. Parents are advised to ensure that their children are only talking to friends and that they aren't being exposed to any adult matter.

SOUND
Sound is crucial in many video games. Players will often wear headphones, meaning parents won't be able to hear what children are listening to. Set up your console or computer to have sound coming from the TV or monitor as well as the headset, so you can hear what your child is experiencing.

REPORTING PLAYERS
If you see or hear a player being abusive, Roblox allows you to report users or interactions. You'll be able to use the Report Abuse links found throughout the site on game pages, but there may also be buttons within chat windows or game menus where you can raise a case with community managers.

SCREEN TIME
Taking regular breaks is important. Set play sessions by using a timer. Some games can last a long time and if your child finishes playing in the middle of a round, they could leave their teammates a player short, and lose any points they've earned. It is advisable to give an advanced warning for stopping play or clearly outlining a stopping point before any play session begins.

IN-GAME PURCHASES
Many games offer in-app purchases to enhance the game experience, but they're not required to play the game. They also don't improve a player's performance. There are ways to set up safety measures on you child's account by setting up a PIN through Settings. Consult these before allowing your child to play any game in order to avoid any unpermitted spending on your account.

Fresh Coriander and Yogurt Dipping Sauce (P)

Coriander is the most widely used herb and features in Indian, Mexican, Chinese, Indonesian, Middle Eastern and Caribbean cooking. It is now generally available in supermarkets.

INGREDIENTS

Serves 4
25g/1oz fresh coriander
1 garlic clove
1 small shallot, chopped finely
120ml/4fl oz/½ cup Greek yogurt
salt and freshly ground black pepper
fresh coriander sprig, to garnish
(optional)

COOK'S TIP

This sauce will keep for 48 hours if stored in a covered container in the fridge.

1 Chop the coriander using a *hachoir* or very sharp knife.

2 Using the flat side of a knife blade, crush the garlic with a little salt to absorb the flavour.

3 Mix the coriander, garlic, shallot and yogurt in a bowl and season to taste with salt and pepper.

4 Spoon into a small serving dish or jar. Serve garnished with a sprig of coriander, if you wish.

Right, clockwise from top left: Fresh Coriander and Yogurt Dipping Sauce, Saffron-flavoured Mayonnaise, Fresh Mayonnaise and Herb-flavoured Mayonnaise.

Fresh Mayonnaise (N)

Fresh mayonnaise is a wonderful, versatile dressing. Since it is a neutral food, it can be used for both starch and protein salads.

INGREDIENTS

Serves 4
2 large egg yolks (preferably free-range)
2.5ml/½ tsp salt
5ml/1 tsp Dijon mustard
5ml/1 tsp finely grated lemon rind (preferably from an unwaxed lemon)
150ml/¼ pint/⅔ cup sunflower oil

VARIATIONS

Add finely chopped mixed fresh herbs, or 2.5ml/½ tsp saffron threads that have been soaked in 15ml/1 tbsp water.

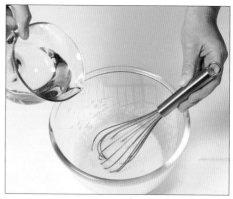

1 Whisk the egg yolks together with the salt, mustard and lemon rind.

2 Add the oil in a slow drizzle, whisking continuously. Do this very slowly at first, so that each drop of oil is incorporated. As the mayonnaise begins to thicken, add the oil in a slow and steady stream. Adjust the seasoning, then spoon the mayonnaise into a serving dish or jar. Mayonnaise can be kept in the fridge for 3–4 days. Serve at room temperature.

Gazpacho Salsa (N)

Freshly made salsa is delicious with simply grilled or barbecued fish. If you can, use home-grown tomatoes for the best flavour. Failing this, pay a little extra for organic tomatoes or buy one of the super-sweet varieties.

INGREDIENTS

Serves 4

¹/₂ large or 1 small cucumber
1 small red onion
450g/1lb firm tomatoes, peeled and seeded
1 large yellow pepper
2 fresh red chillies
1 garlic clove, finely chopped
15ml/1 tbsp finely chopped fresh flat leaf parsley
30ml/2 tbsp finely chopped fresh coriander
30ml/2 tbsp extra virgin olive oil
15ml/1 tbsp cider vinegar
salt and freshly ground black pepper

1 Cut the cucumber in half lengthways. Using a teaspoon, remove and discard the seeds and then cut the flesh into small cubes.

2 Chop the onion and tomatoes into small pieces. Quarter the pepper, discard the seeds and core and cut into small cubes.

3 Finely chop the chillies, discarding the seeds and core.

4 Place all the vegetables in a large bowl and add the garlic, herbs, olive oil, vinegar and seasoning. Mix together thoroughly and then chill in the fridge for 1 hour. Strain off any excess juices and serve.

Anchovy and Parsley Relish (P)

Anchovies and parsley make a flavourful relish to serve as a topping for fresh vegetables.

INGREDIENTS

Serves 4

50g/2oz flat leaf parsley
50g/2oz black olives, stoned
25g/1oz sun-dried tomatoes
4 canned anchovy fillets, drained
50g/2oz red onion, finely chopped
25g/1oz small pickled capers, rinsed
1 garlic clove, finely chopped
15ml/1 tbsp olive oil
juice of ¹/₂ lime
1.5ml/¹/₄ tsp ground black pepper
a selection of cherry tomatoes, celery and cucumber, to serve

1 Coarsely chop the parsley, black olives, sun-dried tomatoes and anchovy fillets and mix in a bowl with the onion, capers, garlic, olive oil, lime juice and black pepper.

2 Halve the cherry tomatoes, cut the celery into bite-size chunks and cut the cucumber into 1cm/¹/₂in slices. Top each of the prepared vegetables with a generous amount of relish and serve.

Italian Rocket and Potato Soup (S)

This filling and hearty soup is based on a traditional Italian peasant recipe. If rocket is unavailable, watercress or baby spinach leaves make an equally delicious alternative.

INGREDIENTS

Serves 4
900g/2lb new potatoes
900ml/1½ pints/3¾ cups well-
  flavoured vegetable stock
1 medium carrot
115g/4oz rocket
2.5ml/½ tsp cayenne pepper
½ loaf stale ciabatta bread, torn
  into chunks
4 garlic cloves, thinly sliced
60ml/4 tbsp olive oil
salt and freshly ground black pepper

1 Dice the potatoes, then place them in a saucepan with the stock and a little salt. Bring to the boil and simmer for 10 minutes.

——————— COOK'S TIP ———————

Garlic burns very easily, so keep your eye on the pan!

2 Finely dice the carrot and add to the potatoes and stock, then tear the rocket leaves and drop into the pan. Simmer for a further 15 minutes, until the vegetables are tender.

3 Add the cayenne pepper and seasoning, then add the chunks of bread. Remove the pan from the heat, then cover and leave to stand for about 10 minutes.

4 Meanwhile sauté the garlic in the olive oil until golden brown. Pour the soup into bowls, add a little of the sautéed garlic to each bowl and serve.

Cream of Grilled Pepper Soup (N)

Weight for weight red and yellow peppers have four times as much Vitamin C as oranges. This is a light, creamy and nutritious soup. Serve with Vegetable Chips instead of Melba toast to serve before a fish main course.

INGREDIENTS

Serves 4

3 large red peppers, halved and seeded
1 large yellow pepper, halved and seeded
15ml/1 tbsp olive oil
1 small shallot, chopped
600ml/1 pint/2½ cups vegetable stock
2 garlic cloves, crushed
1.5ml/¼ tsp saffron strands
150ml/4fl oz/½ cup single cream
475ml/16fl oz/2 cups water
salt and freshly ground black pepper
sprigs of fresh chervil or flat leaf parsley, to garnish
Melba toast, to serve

1 Arrange the peppers skin side up on a baking tray and place under a very hot grill. Grill the peppers until the skin is blackened and blistered and then place them in a plastic bag, knot the end and leave until cool enough to handle. Peel away the skins, reserve one quarter each of a red and yellow pepper and chop the remaining peppers into rough pieces.

2 Heat the oil in a heavy-based saucepan and sauté the shallot until transparent and soft. Add the vegetable stock, garlic, saffron and chopped peppers. Bring to the boil and simmer for 15 minutes.

3 Cool for 10 minutes and then process in a blender or food processor until smooth.

COOK'S TIP

If possible, use home-made vegetable stock, or stock made from a good-quality stock cube or bouillon powder.

4 Return the soup to a clean pan. Mix together the cream and water and add to the soup with salt and pepper. Reheat gently without boiling. Pour the soup into bowls and garnish with thin strips of the reserved peppers and sprigs of chervil or flat leaf parsley. Serve with Melba toast.

Thai Fish Soup (P)

Nam pla is a Thai fish sauce, rich in B vitamins, that is used extensively in Thai cooking. It is available at Thai or Indonesian shops and good supermarkets.

INGREDIENTS

Serves 4

350g/12oz raw large prawns
1 lime
15ml/1 tbsp groundnut oil
1.2 litres/2 pints/5 cups well-flavoured
    chicken or fish stock
1 lemon grass stalk, bruised, cut into
    2.5cm/1in lengths
2 kaffir lime leaves, torn into pieces
½ fresh green chilli, seeded and
    finely sliced
4 scallops
24 mussels, scrubbed
115g/4oz monkfish fillet, cut into
    2cm/¾in chunks
10ml/2 tsp *nam pla*
1 kaffir lime leaf, ½ red chilli, ½ lemon
    grass stalk, all finely sliced, to garnish

1 Peel the prawns, reserving the shells, and remove the black thread along the back. Grate the lime rind and squeeze the juice.

2 Heat the oil in a saucepan and fry the prawn shells until pink. Add the chicken or fish stock, lemon grass, kaffir lime leaves, lime rind and sliced green chilli. Bring to the boil, simmer for 20 minutes and then strain through a fine sieve, reserving the liquid.

3 Prepare the scallops by cutting them in half, leaving the corals attached to one half.

4 Return the stock to a clean pan, add the prawns, mussels, monkfish and scallops and cook for 3 minutes. Remove from the heat and add the lime juice and *nam pla*.

5 Serve garnished with finely sliced red chilli, lemon grass and the kaffir lime leaf.

COOK'S TIP

Double the quantity of fish and seafood to serve as a protein main course.

Star-gazer Vegetable Soup (S)

If you have the time, it is worth making your own stock for this recipe – either vegetable or, if preferred, chicken or fish.

INGREDIENTS

Serves 4
1 yellow pepper
2 large courgettes
2 large carrots
1 kohlrabi
900ml/1½ pints/3¾ cups well-
   flavoured vegetable stock
50g/2oz rice vermicelli
salt and freshly ground black pepper

1 Cut the pepper into quarters, removing the seeds and core. Cut the courgettes and carrots lengthways into 5mm/¼in slices and slice the kohlrabi into 5mm/¼in rounds.

2 Using tiny pastry cutters, stamp out shapes from the vegetables or use a very sharp knife to fashion the sliced vegetables into stars, and other decorative shapes.

COOK'S TIP

Sauté the remaining vegetable pieces in a little oil and mix with cooked brown rice to make a tasty risotto.

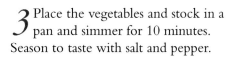

3 Place the vegetables and stock in a pan and simmer for 10 minutes. Season to taste with salt and pepper.

4 Meanwhile, place the vermicelli in a bowl, cover with boiling water and set aside for 4 minutes. Drain, divide among four warmed soup bowls and ladle over the soup.

FISH AND SEAFOOD

Although most fish and seafood are available all year round, many varieties have a natural season when they are plentiful and have the best flavour. You don't need masses of other ingredients to make fish as wonderfully different as roasted cod with its smooth fresh tomato sauce or grilled salmon served with a super-easy yogurt sauce subtly flavoured with fresh mint and cucumber. Whole sea bass baked "en papillote" is simplicity itself – the paper parcel conserves all its aromatic juices, which are released only as you serve the fish.

Roasted Cod with Fresh Tomato Sauce (P)

Really fresh cod has a sweet, delicate flavour and a pure white flaky flesh. Served with an aromatic tomato sauce, it provides a nutritious meal.

INGREDIENTS

Serves 4
350g/12oz fresh ripe plum tomatoes
75ml/5 tbsp olive oil
2.5ml/½ tsp caster sugar
2 strips of orange rind
1 fresh thyme sprig
6 fresh basil leaves
900g/2lb fresh cod fillet with skin
salt and freshly ground black pepper
steamed green beans, to serve

1 Preheat the oven to 230°C/450°F/ Gas 8. Roughly chop the tomatoes.

2 Heat 15ml/1 tbsp of the olive oil in a heavy-based saucepan, add the tomatoes, sugar, orange rind, thyme and basil and simmer for 5 minutes until the tomatoes are soft.

3 Press the tomato mixture through a fine sieve, discarding the tomato skins and seeds, orange rind and hard pieces of thyme. Pour into a small saucepan and heat gently.

4 Scale the cod fillet and cut on the diagonal into four equal pieces. Season well with salt and pepper.

5 Heat the remaining oil in a clean heavy-based frying pan and fry the cod, skin side down, until the skin is crisp. Place the fish on a greased baking sheet, skin side up, and roast in the oven for 8–10 minutes until the fish is cooked through. Serve the fish on the steamed green beans with the tomato sauce drizzled over it.

Haddock in Spinach Parcels with Pepper Purée (P)

This recipe really deserves a freshly made fish stock, but stock made from vegetable bouillon powder is preferable to most stock cubes. It is delicious served with a sweet pepper purée.

INGREDIENTS

Serves 4

15ml/1 tbsp olive oil
1 small shallot, sliced
2 garlic cloves, sliced
2 yellow peppers, seeded and chopped
1 fresh thyme sprig
600ml/1 pint/2½ cups fish stock
50ml/2fl oz/¼ cup double cream
4 fresh haddock fillets, about 175g/6oz each, skinned
8 large spinach leaves, blanched
salt and freshly ground black pepper

1 Heat the oil in a heavy-based pan and fry the shallot and garlic for 3 minutes, stirring frequently. Add the peppers, thyme and 475ml/16fl oz/ 2 cups of the fish stock. Season with salt and pepper, then simmer for 15 minutes until the peppers are tender.

COOK'S TIP

To blanch spinach leaves, place them in a colander and pour over boiling water. Plunge them immediately into ice-cold water to set the colour.

2 Place the pepper mixture in a blender or food processor, then process until smooth. Stir in the cream, then pour into a clean saucepan and heat gently to warm through.

3 Meanwhile, half-wrap each fish fillet in two of the blanched spinach leaves. Place the remaining stock in a pan and bring to the boil. Place the fish packages in a steamer, season, then set over the stock and steam for 4 minutes. Arrange the fish parcels on four warmed serving plates and serve with the warm sauce.

Stuffed Sardines with Fresh Rosemary (P)

If fresh sardines are not available, choose four small herrings or two mackerel – they are also delicious cooked this way.

INGREDIENTS

Serves 4
15ml/1 tbsp olive oil
1.5kg/3lb fresh sardines
1 large sprig fresh rosemary
45ml/3 tbsp chopped fresh parsley
1 shallot, finely chopped
115g/4oz/1 cup pine nuts
2 garlic cloves, finely chopped
juice and finely grated rind of
   1 large lemon
salt and freshly ground black pepper
lemon wedges and sprigs of fresh
   rosemary, to garnish

1 Preheat the oven to 190°C/375°F/ Gas 5 and brush an ovenproof dish with a little of the olive oil. Remove the heads of the sardines and split each one down the belly.

2 Place the fish on a chopping board, cut side down, and gently but firmly press down on the backbone. Turn them over and ease out the backbone. Wash the fish well in salted water and pat dry.

3 Pull away the rosemary leaves from the stem and chop finely. Place in a bowl and mix with the parsley, shallot, pine nuts and garlic.

4 Season the fish inside and out with salt and pepper and place a spoonful or two of stuffing inside each one. Press the sides around the stuffing and place each fish in the baking dish.

5 Sprinkle over the remaining olive oil and bake for 30 minutes. Just before serving, squeeze over the lemon juice and sprinkle with the lemon rind. Garnish with lemon wedges and sprigs of rosemary.

Fried Monkfish with Home-made Tapenade (P)

INGREDIENTS

Serves 3–4
450g/1lb fresh monkfish fillet
30ml/2 tbsp olive oil
salt and freshly ground black pepper
chopped fresh parsley and diced red
   pepper, to garnish

For the tapenade
450g/1lb black olives, stoned
75g/3oz capers, drained and rinsed
75g/3oz canned anchovy fillets,
   drained and diced
15ml/1 tbsp Dijon mustard
10 fresh basil leaves, roughly torn
4 garlic cloves, crushed
about 120ml/4fl oz/½ cup extra virgin
   olive oil
15ml/1 tbsp brandy
2.5ml/½ tsp freshly ground
   black pepper

1 To make the tapenade, place all the ingredients in a blender or food processor and process until the mixture is well blended but still has a little texture, adding a little extra olive oil if necessary. You will need about half of the mixture for this recipe – store the remainder in the fridge in a screw-top jar.

2 Cut the fish into rounds about 2.5cm/1in thick. Season with salt and pepper.

3 Heat the olive oil in a heavy-based frying pan and fry the fish on one side for 2 minutes. Turn the fish over and cook for a further 1 minute.

4 Place a generous spoonful of tapenade in the centre of four serving plates and arrange the fish around each mound. Sprinkle with parsley and diced red pepper and serve.

Whole Sea Bass en Papillote (P)

Sea bass is also known as sea wolf, sea dace or sea perch and has delicate pink flesh and a light sweet smell. Cooking in baking paper means the fish retains its flavour. Mullet and bream can be cooked in the same way.

INGREDIENTS

Serves 4

1.5kg/3–3½lb fresh whole sea bass, cleaned, scaled and head removed
5 fresh mint sprigs
½ lemon, sliced
2 shallots, finely sliced
2 fresh plum tomatoes, sliced
45ml/3 tbsp olive oil
salt and freshly ground black pepper
steamed broccoli, to serve

1 Preheat the oven to 175°C/350°F/ Gas 4. Wash and dry the fish and place on a double piece of non-stick baking paper, large enough to wrap the fish comfortably.

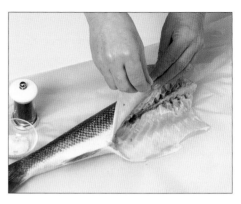

2 Season the fish inside and out with salt and pepper.

3 Tuck the fresh mint sprigs, lemon slices, shallots and tomato slices inside the fish and drizzle the olive oil over its back.

4 Fold the paper over the fish and double fold the three open edges.

5 Place the fish on a baking sheet and bake for 40–50 minutes until cooked through. Cut the package open with scissors and serve the fish with steamed broccoli.

Salmon with Yogurt and Mint Dressing (P)

Salmon is a very rich fish and is delicious, grilled and served with this light and delicate sauce. A mixed green leaf and herb salad makes a perfect accompaniment.

INGREDIENTS

Serves 4

½ large cucumber
6 fresh mint leaves
150ml/¼ pint/⅔ cup natural
  Greek yogurt
675g/1½ lb fresh salmon fillet, middle
  cut with skin
5ml/1 tsp olive oil
salt and freshly ground black pepper
mint sprigs, to garnish
fresh spinach leaves, to serve

1 Peel the cucumber, slice in half lengthways and remove the seeds.

2 Grate the cucumber into a sieve, salt lightly and drain for about 30 minutes. Chop the mint leaves.

3 Place the chopped mint leaves in a bowl with the yogurt. Squeeze out any excess juice from the cucumber and stir into the bowl with the yogurt and mint. Season with black pepper.

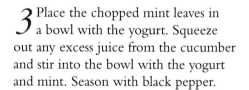

4 Preheat the grill until moderately hot. Scale the salmon if the fishmonger has not already done this and check for any bones. Cut the salmon into four pieces, brush with the olive oil and season with a little salt.

5 Grill the fish for 3 minutes, skin side up, then carefully turn over the fish and grill for about 2 minutes on the other side. The skin should be browned and crisp. Serve on a bed of spinach with the yogurt and cucumber dressing. Garnish with sprigs of mint and grind over some black pepper.

Butterflied Mediterranean Prawns (P)

Skewered prawns, marinated in a fiery herb dressing, then grilled until pink and tender, make a delicious light lunch or summer supper dish.

INGREDIENTS

Serves 4
32 raw king prawns, peeled
2 garlic cloves, finely chopped
90ml/6 tbsp finely chopped fresh parsley
1 fresh rosemary sprig, leaves removed and finely chopped
pinch of dried chilli flakes
juice of 2 fresh limes
30ml/2 tbsp olive oil
salt and freshly ground black pepper
green salad, to serve

1 Wash the prawns in salted water, remove their heads and shells, then remove the black thread that runs along the back of the prawn. To butterfly the prawns, cut along the back, without completely cutting through, then carefully fan out.

2 Blend the garlic, parsley, rosemary, chilli flakes, lime juice and olive oil in a large bowl. Add the prawns, stir well and leave to marinate for 1 hour.

3 Meanwhile, soak 32 wooden skewers in warm water for at least 30 minutes.

4 Preheat the grill until very hot. Thread 2 prawns on to each pair of skewers and grill for 2–3 minutes until each side has turned bright pink. Remove the prawns from the skewers and serve with green salad.

Seared Scallops with Lemon and Thyme (P)

Scallop shells make attractive little dishes and most good fishmongers will sell you the scallops and shells together. Make sure the shells are well scrubbed and clean before using.

INGREDIENTS

Serves 4
50ml/2fl oz/¼ cup olive oil
2 garlic cloves, finely chopped
4 fresh thyme sprigs
1 bay leaf
15ml/1 tbsp chopped fresh parsley
16 fresh scallops, rinsed
1 shallot, finely chopped
15ml/1 tbsp balsamic vinegar
30ml/2 tbsp lemon juice
150ml/¼ pint/⅔ cup chicken or vegetable stock
salt and freshly ground black pepper
24 baby spinach leaves, to garnish

1 Blend the olive oil, garlic, thyme, bay leaf and parsley in a shallow bowl. Add the scallops and leave to marinate in a cool place for 1 hour.

2 Heat a heavy-based frying pan until smoking. Remove the scallops from the marinade and sear for about 30 seconds on each side to seal in their juices. Transfer the scallops to a plate and keep warm.

3 Add the marinade to the pan, then add the shallot and balsamic vinegar, lemon juice and stock. Cook over a high heat for 5 minutes until the stock is well reduced. Discard the bay leaf and season with salt and pepper.

4 Arrange 6 spinach leaves around each scallop shell in the centre of four serving plates, place 4 scallops in each shell and pour over the juices.

Mussels in Fennel and White Wine (P)

INGREDIENTS

Serves 4

1.5kg/3–3½lb fresh mussels
3 shallots
3 garlic cloves
1 small fennel bulb
15ml/1 tbsp olive oil
300ml/½ pint/1¼ cups dry white wine
15ml/1 tbsp chopped fresh parsley
juice of ½ lemon
chopped fresh parsley, to garnish
salt and freshly ground black pepper

COOK'S TIP

After you have washed the mussels, give any that are open a sharp tap, and if they refuse to close, discard them. Conversely, any mussels that remain closed after cooking should also be thrown away.

---

1 Scrub the mussels thoroughly in several changes of water (see Cook's Tip) and pull away the beards. Set the mussles aside.

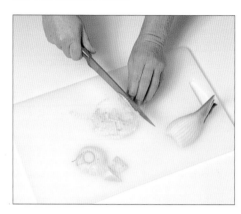

2 Finely chop the shallots and garlic. Remove the root from the fennel and slice finely.

3 Heat the oil in a heavy-based pan and fry the shallots, fennel and garlic for 1 minute, stirring all the time. Add the wine and simmer for 5 minutes.

4 Add the mussels and parsley, cover with a tight-fitting lid and cook for 4 minutes, shaking the pan occasionally. Remove the lid and check that all the mussels are open.

5 Squeeze in the lemon juice, then season to taste. Divide the mussels among four large bowls. Pour the liquid over the mussels and sprinkle with chopped parsley.

Seafarer's Stew (P)

Any variety of firm fish may be used in this recipe, but be sure to use smoked haddock as well; it is essential for its distinctive flavour.

INGREDIENTS

Serves 4

225g/8oz naturally smoked haddock
   fillet (uncoloured)
225g/8oz fresh monkfish fillet
20 fresh mussels, scrubbed
2 streaky bacon rashers (optional)
15ml/1 tbsp olive oil
1 shallot, finely chopped
225g/8oz carrots, coarsely grated
150ml/¼ pint/⅔ cup single or
   double cream
115g/4oz cooked peeled prawns
salt and freshly ground black pepper
30ml/2 tbsp chopped fresh parsley,
   to garnish

1 In a large heavy-based pan, simmer the haddock and monkfish in 1.2 litres/2 pints/5 cups water for 5 minutes, then add the mussels and cover the pan with a lid.

2 Cook for a further 5 minutes or until all the mussels have opened. Discard any that have not. Drain, reserving the liquid. Return the liquid to the rinsed pan and set aside.

3 Flake the haddock coarsely, removing any skin and bones, then cut the monkfish into large chunks. Cut the bacon, if using, into strips.

4 Heat the oil in a heavy-based frying pan and fry the shallot and bacon for 3–4 minutes or until the shallot is soft and the bacon lightly browned. Add to the strained fish broth, bring to the boil, then add the grated carrots and cook for 10 minutes.

5 Stir in the cream together with the haddock, monkfish, mussels and prawns and heat gently, without boiling. Season and serve in large bowls, garnished with parsley.

COOK'S TIP

The advantage of using double cream is that the liquid will not curdle if you do accidentally let it boil.

VEGETABLES AND SALADS

Vegetables and salads are vital to healthy eating and should be considered as an important part of each meal and not just an occasional accompaniment. For the finest flavour, choose organic and seasonal varieties whenever possible. Stoved Mixed Mushrooms are a meal in themselves served in a hollowed out wholemeal bread roll and accompanied by lots of fresh salad. Celeriac, Turnip and Carrot Purée is delicious to mop up the juices of fish or game, and makes a nutritious meal on its own served with nutty brown rice generously scattered with toasted hazelnuts.

Winter Vegetable Ragout (S)

INGREDIENTS

Serves 4

30ml/2 tbsp extra virgin olive oil
1 onion, finely chopped
25g/1oz dried porcini mushrooms,
   rinsed well, then soaked in 300ml/
   ½ pint/1¼ cups hot water
   for 10 minutes
2 garlic cloves, finely chopped
1 fresh thyme sprig
2 bay leaves
4 carrots, cut into 5cm/2in sticks
1 celery stick, sliced
1 small cauliflower, broken
   into florets
2 parsnips, cut into 5cm/2in sticks
2 large potatoes, cubed
115g/4oz button mushrooms
115g/4oz baby Brussels sprouts
salt and freshly ground black pepper
30ml/2 tbsp each chopped fresh parsley
   and tarragon, to garnish

1 Heat the olive oil in a large heavy-based frying pan and fry the onion for 4–5 minutes until golden brown. Drain the mushrooms, reserving the soaking liquid.

2 Add the garlic, thyme, bay leaves, carrots, celery, cauliflower, parsnips and potatoes. Stir well and cook for 2 minutes.

3 Strain the mushroom liquid and add to the pan together with the porcini mushrooms. Cover and cook gently for 10 minutes.

4 Add the button mushrooms and Brussels sprouts and cook for a further 5 minutes until all of the vegetables are tender. Taste and adjust the seasoning, then serve, with the chopped parsley and tarragon sprinkled over the top.

COOK'S TIP

Turn the ragout into a pie by covering it with a thick layer of mashed potatoes. Bake in the oven at 180°C/350°F/Gas 4 for a further 30 minutes until the potatoes are golden brown.

Almost-dry Roasted Vegetables (N)

This is a delicious if rather slow method of cooking vegetables, but they retain all their juicy flavour. Serve them with pasta, hot toast or Grilled Polenta as a starch main course.

INGREDIENTS

Serves 4
1 aubergine
2 courgettes
1 yellow pepper
1 red pepper
4 garlic cloves
1 sweet red onion
1 small fennel bulb
20 small asparagus spears
10 fresh basil leaves, roughly torn
45ml/3 tbsp extra virgin olive oil
15ml/1 tbsp balsamic vinegar
salt and freshly ground black pepper
sprigs of basil, to garnish

1 Preheat the oven to 240°C/475°F/ Gas 9. Cut the aubergine and courgettes into 1cm/½in slices. Halve the peppers, discard the seeds and core, then cut them into chunks.

2 Finely chop the garlic and cut the onion into eight wedges.

3 Remove the root from the fennel and slice into 2.5cm/1in strips.

4 Place all the vegetables in a bowl, add the basil, then stir in the olive oil. Season with salt and pepper and mix together well.

5 Tip the vegetables into a shallow roasting dish and roast in the oven for 30–40 minutes until the vegetables are brown on the edges. Leave to cool, then sprinkle with the balsamic vinegar and serve garnished with sprigs of basil.

Celeriac, Turnip and Carrot Purée (N)

This sophisticated, subtly coloured combination of root vegetables is delicious with both meat and fish. Parsnips and swede have stronger flavours and are excellent with pheasant and pork.

INGREDIENTS

Serves 4
225g/8oz celeriac
225g/8oz turnips
225g/8oz carrots
1 small shallot
25g/1oz/2 tbsp butter
15ml/1 tbsp single cream
1.5ml/¼ tsp freshly grated nutmeg
salt and freshly ground black pepper
fresh chives, to garnish

1 Peel the celeriac and peel or scrape the turnips if necessary.

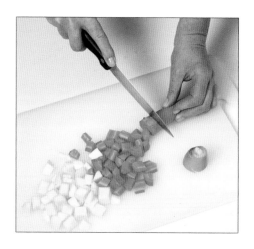

2 Cut the celeriac, turnips and carrots into bite-size pieces and finely chop the shallot. Place in a pan of very lightly salted boiling water. Cook for 8 minutes until tender but still firm.

3 Drain in a colander and place in a blender or food processor with the butter and cream. Process to a fine purée, then season with salt, pepper and nutmeg. Spoon directly into four serving bowls. Garnish with fresh chives and serve immediately.

Stir-fried Green Beans with Ginger (N)

Green beans keep their crunchy texture even after cooking and may be served cold as an alternative salad or as a tasty light starter.

INGREDIENTS

Serves 4
1cm/½in piece fresh root ginger
450g/1lb fresh green beans
30ml/2 tbsp olive oil
2.5ml/½ tsp black mustard seeds
50ml/2fl oz/¼ cup water
2.5ml/½ tsp ground cumin
1.5ml/¼ tsp ground turmeric
30ml/2 tbsp chopped fresh coriander
5ml/1 tsp salt
5ml/1 tsp lemon juice
freshly ground black pepper
shreds of fried ginger, to garnish

1 Peel the ginger and cut into very fine strips. Top and tail the beans and cut in half.

2 Heat the olive oil in a large frying pan, wok or flameproof casserole and sauté the mustard seeds and ginger until the seeds crackle.

3 Add the beans and stir-fry over a medium heat for 5 minutes.

4 Add the water, cover the pan and simmer for 3 minutes. Remove the lid and simmer until almost all the water has evaporated, then add the cumin, turmeric, coriander and salt.

5 Continue cooking until the beans are tender but crisp, and the water has completely evaporated. Add the lemon juice, season with black pepper and garnish with shreds of ginger. Serve at once.

COOK'S TIP

Be careful not to allow the beans to overcook or they will lose their delicious crunchy texture.

Stoved Mixed Mushrooms (S)

Nothing can match the flavour of freshly picked wild mushrooms: the next best thing is to combine several different cultivated types. If possible, choose organically grown mushrooms, which have a richer flavour.

INGREDIENTS

Serves 4

2 garlic cloves
1 shallot
450g/1lb mushrooms, such as oyster, brown-cap, large field, button and ceps
75ml/5 tbsp olive oil
30ml/2 tbsp chopped fresh chervil
30ml/2 tbsp chopped fresh parsley
chopped leaves of 1 fresh rosemary sprig
salt and freshly ground black pepper
sprigs of fresh chervil, to garnish
4 bread rolls, to serve

1 Finely chop the garlic and shallot. Wipe the mushrooms, carefully removing any dirt and discarding any very tough stems. Slice the larger mushrooms and halve the smaller ones.

2 Heat the olive oil in a heavy-based, deep frying pan and fry the shallot over a medium to high heat for about 1 minute.

3 Add the garlic, mushrooms and fresh herbs to the pan and sauté for about 5 minutes. Season to taste. Split open the bread rolls by cutting a cross in the top, then divide the mushrooms among them. Garnish with sprigs of chervil and serve.

--- VARIATION ---

For an alternative substantial starch meal, serve the mushrooms with Grilled Polenta or freshly cooked pasta. Served without the bread rolls, this dish is neutral and would make a tasty starter before either a starch or protein main course.

Aubergine and Spinach Terrines (P)

These individual terrines make an elegant first course or accompaniment to either a fish or meat course, cold or hot.

INGREDIENTS

Serves 4

1 aubergine
30ml/2 tbsp extra virgin olive oil
2 courgettes, thinly sliced
leaves from 1 small fresh thyme sprig
4 firm tomatoes, peeled and seeded
4 fresh basil leaves, finely sliced
275g/10oz baby spinach leaves
1 garlic clove, crushed
15g/½oz/1 tbsp butter
pinch of freshly grated nutmeg
salt and freshly ground black pepper
½ roasted red pepper, skinned and
   chopped, plus a little balsamic
   vinegar, to serve

1 Preheat the oven to 190°C/375°F/ Gas 5 and seal four 6cm/2½in diameter metal muffin rings at one end with clear film.

2 Slice the aubergine into four equal-sized rounds. Heat half the oil in a frying pan and fry the aubergines on both sides until brown. Place the aubergines on a baking sheet and cook in the oven for 10 minutes. Transfer to a plate lined with kitchen paper.

3 Heat half the remaining oil in the same pan and fry the courgettes for 2 minutes, then drain on the kitchen paper. Season with salt and pepper and sprinkle with thyme leaves.

4 Place the tomatoes, basil and the rest of the oil in a heavy-based frying pan and cook for 5–8 minutes. Cook the spinach, garlic and butter in a saucepan, allowing all the water to evaporate. Drain and add the nutmeg and season with salt and pepper.

5 Line the base and about 1cm/½ in of the sides of the muffin rings with the spinach leaves, making sure the leaves overlap, leaving no gaps. Place the courgettes around the edges of each ring, overlapping slightly.

6 Divide the tomato mixture equally among the rings, pressing down well. Place the aubergines on the top, trimming the edges to fit.

7 Seal the top with clear film and pierce the base to allow any liquid to escape. Chill overnight. Remove carefully from the rings and serve with diced roasted peppers, drizzled with balsamic vinegar.

COOK'S TIP

Double or triple the quantities in this recipe to make a vegetarian main course and serve with a crisp green salad and a sharp lemon and oil dressing.

Mixed Green Leaf and Herb Salad (N)

Serve this salad as an accompaniment, or turn it into a main course salad by adding one of the variations, right.

INGREDIENTS

Serves 4

15g/¹/₂oz/¹/₂ cup mixed fresh herbs, such as chervil, tarragon (use sparingly), dill, basil, marjoram (use sparingly), flat leaf parsley, mint, sorrel, fennel and coriander
350g/12oz mixed salad leaves, such as rocket, radicchio, chicory, watercress, curly endive, baby spinach, oakleaf lettuce, nasturtium (and the flowers) and dandelion

For the dressing

50ml/2fl oz/¹/₄ cup extra virgin olive oil
15ml/1 tbsp sherry vinegar
salt and freshly ground black pepper

1 Wash and dry the herbs and salad leaves using a salad spinner or place them between two clean, dry dish towels and carefully pat dry.

2 Blend together the oil and vinegar and season well.

3 Place the salad and herbs in a large bowl, add the dressing and mix well using your hands to toss the leaves. The dressing should be added just before serving.

VARIATIONS

For a protein main course, add one of the following:
• Freshly grilled salmon or tuna or cooked peeled prawns, either cold or grilled, and lightly dusted with chilli powder.
• Fat slices of mozzarella cheese with stoned black olives and a few green capers.
• Slivers of Pecorino cheese with bite-size pieces of crisp pear.

For a starch main course, add one of the following:
• Tiny new potatoes in their jackets, crumbled hard-boiled egg yolks, sprouted beansprouts.
• Baby broad beans, sliced artichoke hearts and garlic croûtons.
• Cooked chick-peas, asparagus tips and stoned green olives stuffed with peppers.

Feta and Apple Salad (P)

INGREDIENTS

Serves 4

45ml/3 tbsp olive oil
juice of 1 lime
1.5ml/¹/₂ tsp English mustard
1 red apple
1 green apple
50g/2oz rocket
400g/14oz freshly sprouted seeds and pulses
2 spring onions, finely chopped
5ml/1 tsp chopped fresh basil
10ml/2 tsp snipped fresh chives
10ml/2 tsp chopped fresh chervil
5ml/1 tsp chopped fresh tarragon
30ml/2 tbsp chopped walnuts
175g/6oz feta cheese
salt and freshly ground black pepper

1 Pour the olive oil and lime juice into a large bowl and mix with the mustard, salt and black pepper.

VARIATION

As an alternative to feta, which is rather salty, you could use a milder but still crumbly cheese like Caerphilly.

2 Core the apples, slice into thin shavings and mix with the dressing in the bowl. Add the rocket, sprouted seeds and pulses, spring onions, herbs and walnuts and mix well.

3 Serve in one large serving bowl or in four individual bowls with the feta cheese crumbled on top.

Oriental Salad (N)

This fragrantly flavoured salad combines with either starch or protein meals. The dressing may be used for any combinations of raw vegetables and green salads.

INGREDIENTS

Serves 4

225g/8oz fresh beansprouts
1 cucumber
2 carrots
1 small daikon radish
1 small red onion, thinly sliced
2.5cm/1in fresh root ginger, peeled and
    cut into thin matchsticks
1 small red chilli, seeded and
    thinly sliced
handful of fresh coriander leaves or
    fresh mint leaves

For the oriental dressing

15ml/1 tbsp rice vinegar
15ml/1 tbsp light soy sauce
15ml/1 tbsp *nam pla* (Thai fish sauce)
1 garlic clove, finely chopped
15ml/1 tbsp sesame oil
45ml/3 tbsp groundnut oil
30ml/2 tbsp sesame seeds,
    lightly toasted

1 First make the dressing. Place all the dressing ingredients in a bottle or screw-top jar and shake well.

2 Wash the beansprouts and drain thoroughly in a colander.

3 Peel the cucumber, cut in half lengthways and scoop out the seeds. Peel the cucumber flesh into long ribbon strips using a potato peeler or mandolin.

4 Peel the carrots and radish into long strips in the same way as for the cucumber.

5 Place the carrots, radish and cucumber in a large shallow serving dish, add the onion, ginger, chilli and coriander or mint and toss to mix. Pour the dressing over just before serving.

----- COOK'S TIP -----

The dressing may be made in advance and will keep well for a couple of days if stored in the fridge or a cool place.

Fennel and Herb Coleslaw (N)

This neutral salad may be adapted into a protein meal with the addition of generous chunks of feta or any other crumbly and salty cheese together with slices of crisp red apples.

INGREDIENTS

Serves 4

175g/6oz fennel
2 spring onions
175g/6oz white cabbage
115g/4oz celery
175g/6oz carrots
50g/2oz sultanas
2.5ml/½ tsp caraway seeds (optional)
15ml/1 tbsp chopped fresh parsley
45ml/3 tbsp extra virgin olive oil
5ml/1 tsp lemon juice
shreds of spring onion, to garnish

1 Using a sharp knife, cut the fennel and spring onions into thin slices.

VARIATION

Use soured cream instead of olive oil for a creamier dressing.

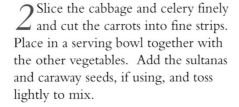

2 Slice the cabbage and celery finely and cut the carrots into fine strips. Place in a serving bowl together with the other vegetables. Add the sultanas and caraway seeds, if using, and toss lightly to mix.

3 Stir in the chopped parsley, olive oil and lemon juice and mix all the ingredients very thoroughly. Cover and chill for 3 hours to allow the flavours to mingle, and then serve, garnished with spring onion shreds.

GRAINS, PULSES AND RICE

If you have always thought of grains and pulses as rather dull and stodgy you will be pleasantly surprised by the flavour and texture of Cracked Wheat Salad and Bean Feast with its sharp and pungent Tomato and Avocado Salsa. Freshly made Hummus is much more wholesome and crunchy when made with sprouted chick-peas and is irresistible with lots of piping hot Vegetable Chips. While all these recipes are indicated as starch dishes, beans and pulses do contain some protein which is important for vegetarians.

Falafels with Tahini Dressing (S)

Falafels or chick-pea rissoles are a popular Middle Eastern snack. Serve them with a green leaf salad and pitta bread.

INGREDIENTS

Serves 4

225g/8oz/1½ cups dried chick-peas, soaked overnight
1 large onion, finely chopped
4 spring onions, finely chopped
45ml/3 tbsp chopped fresh coriander
45ml/3 tbsp chopped fresh parsley
5ml/1 tsp ground coriander
5ml/1 tsp ground fennel seeds
5ml/1 tsp ground cumin
2.5ml/½ tsp baking powder
2 garlic cloves, crushed
sunflower oil, for frying
salt and freshly ground black pepper
pinch of paprika and chopped fresh coriander, to garnish

For the dressing
45ml/3 tbsp tahini

1 Drain the chick-peas and cook in plenty of boiling water for 1–1½ hours until tender.

2 Drain the chick-peas and process in a blender or food processor until they form a smooth paste. Add the onion and spring onions, coriander and parsley, process again for a few seconds and then add the ground spices, baking powder and crushed garlic. Season with salt and pepper.

3 Tip the mixture into a bowl and knead with your hands until pliable, then leave it to rest in the fridge for at least 30 minutes.

4 Meanwhile, make the dressing. Place the tahini in a bowl and gradually add 120ml/4fl oz/½ cup water, to make a smooth paste, the consistency of cream. Season with salt and pepper and spoon into a serving bowl. Chill until ready to serve.

5 Take walnut-size pieces of the mixture and form into small balls about 4cm/1½in across. Heat a little oil in a frying pan and fry the falafels, three or four at a time, for about 3 minutes each side, until lightly browned. Drain on kitchen paper and keep warm. Repeat with the remaining falafels. Arrange on a serving plate, dust with paprika and garnish with fresh coriander. Serve with the tahini dressing.

Hummus with Baked Vegetable Chips (S)

This classic Middle Eastern starter is ideally made using sprouted chick-peas, which are available at health food stores and most good supermarkets. Canned chick-peas are a useful standby and can be used in place of the sprouted chick-peas – rinse them thoroughly before using.

INGREDIENTS

Serves 4
450g/1lb sprouted chick-peas (or 400g/14oz can chick-peas)
2 garlic cloves, crushed
60ml/4 tbsp tahini
60ml/4 tbsp extra virgin olive oil
30ml/2 tbsp lemon juice
salt
small pinch of paprika and sprigs of flat leaf parsley or chervil, to garnish

For the vegetable chips
2 large aubergines
4 large parsnips
5ml/1 tsp extra virgin olive oil

1 Blend the chick-peas in a food processor until completely smooth. Add the garlic, tahini and a little salt.

COOK'S TIP

To make a rich sauce for steamed vegetables, just add a little more water.

2 With the machine running, slowly pour on the olive oil to make a thick, smooth sauce and then add the lemon juice. If the mixture is too thick, add a little water. Transfer to a serving bowl and set aside in a cool place.

3 Preheat the oven to 120°C/250°F/ Gas ½. Slice the aubergines and parsnips into very thin rounds. Brush both sides of the vegetable slices with olive oil and sprinkle with a little salt.

4 Place on oven racks and bake in the oven for 30 minutes until golden brown and crisp. The vegetables may take longer, so continue cooking, checking every 10 minutes.

5 Serve the vegetable chips with the hummus, garnished with a light dusting of paprika and sprigs of fresh parsley or chervil.

Cracked Wheat Salad with Walnuts and Herbs (S)

INGREDIENTS

Serves 4

225g/8oz/1 generous cup cracked
  wheat
350ml/12fl oz/1½ cups vegetable stock
1 cinnamon stick
generous pinch of ground cumin
pinch of cayenne pepper
pinch of ground cloves
5ml/1 tsp salt, finely ground
10 mangetouts, topped and tailed
1 red and 1 yellow pepper, roasted,
  skinned, seeded and diced
2 plum tomatoes, peeled, seeded
  and diced
2 shallots, finely sliced
5 black olives, stoned and cut
  into quarters
30ml/2 tbsp each shredded fresh basil,
  mint and parsley
30ml/2 tbsp roughly chopped walnuts
30ml/2 tbsp balsamic vinegar
120ml/4fl oz/½ cup extra virgin
  olive oil
freshly ground black pepper
onion rings, to garnish

1 Place the cracked wheat in a large bowl. Pour the stock into a saucepan and bring to the boil with the spices and salt.

2 Cook for 1 minute, then pour the stock over the cracked wheat and leave to stand for 30 minutes.

COOK'S TIP

To roast the peppers, cut in half and place skin side up on a baking tray. Place in an oven preheated to 220°C/425°F/Gas 7 and roast for about 20 minutes until the skins are charred. Place the peppers in a plastic bag, knot the end and leave for 10 minutes. The skin will then be simply pulled away.

3 In another bowl, mix together the mangetouts, peppers, tomatoes, shallots, olives, herbs and walnuts. Add the vinegar, olive oil and a little black pepper and stir thoroughly to mix.

4 Strain the cracked wheat of any liquid and discard the cinnamon stick. Place in a serving bowl, stir in the fresh vegetable mixture and serve, garnished with onion rings.

Savoy Cabbage and Vegetable Pie (S)

Before cooking the lentils, spread them out on a plate to check there are no pieces of grit, which often occur and can seriously damage your teeth! Serve this pie with baked potatoes, or new potatoes steamed in their jackets.

INGREDIENTS

Serves 4

1 small Savoy cabbage, outer leaves removed
45ml/3 tbsp olive oil
1 shallot, finely chopped
1 garlic clove, finely chopped
1 carrot, cut into small dice
1 leek, white part only, cut into thin slices
1 celery stick, cut into small dice
15ml/1 tbsp pine nuts
1 bay leaf
115g/4oz/½ cup Puy lentils
600ml/1 pint/2½ cups vegetable stock
75ml/5 tbsp double cream
3 egg yolks
salt and freshly ground black pepper

1 Pull away ten large undamaged cabbage leaves and blanch them in a saucepan of boiling water for 1 minute. Plunge into a bowl of ice-cold water for 30 seconds and drain immediately.

2 Cut the remaining cabbage into quarters, cut out and discard the stalk and slice very thinly.

3 Heat the oil in a heavy-based saucepan and fry the shallot for 3 minutes until softened. Add the garlic, sliced cabbage, carrot, leek, celery, pine nuts and bay leaf and cook for a further 3 minutes, stirring frequently.

4 Add the lentils and vegetable stock to the pan, cover and simmer for about 30 minutes until the lentils are tender and the liquid has evaporated. Leave to cool. Preheat the oven to 200°C/400°F/Gas 6.

5 Line a 15cm/6in flan tin with seven of the cabbage leaves and season with salt and pepper.

6 Blend the cream with the egg yolks and stir into the lentil mixture. Season to taste, then spoon the mixture into the cabbage ring and cover with the remaining leaves. Cover with foil and cook in the oven for 40 minutes. Once the pie is cooked, leave it to stand, still covered with foil, for 10 minutes before slicing into thick wedges to serve.

Wild Rice and Grain Pilaf with Mushrooms (S)

INGREDIENTS

Serves 4

50g/2oz/¼ cup wheat berries
25g/1oz/2 tbsp butter
1 shallot, finely chopped
50g/2oz/¼ cup wild rice
600ml/1 pint/2½ cups vegetable stock
1 bay leaf
50g/2oz/¼ cup brown basmati rice
115g/4oz/1½ cups shiitake mushrooms
115g/4oz/1½ cups brown-cap
  mushrooms
30ml/2 tbsp olive oil
4 spring onions, thinly sliced
50g/2oz/¼ cup hazelnuts, roughly
  chopped
salt and freshly ground black pepper

1 Rinse the wheat berries, cover with 1 litre/1¾ pints/4 cups boiling water and leave to soak for at least 2 hours or overnight. Drain.

2 Melt the butter in a heavy-based frying pan and fry the shallot for 3 minutes. Add the wheat berries and wild rice, stir well to coat the grains, and then add the stock, bay leaf and 2.5ml/½ tsp salt. Bring to the boil, then lower the heat, cover and simmer for 30 minutes.

3 Stir in the brown basmati rice and simmer for a further 20 minutes. Remove from the heat and leave to stand for 5 minutes.

4 Quarter the shiitake mushrooms and remove and discard the stem. Quarter the brown-cap mushrooms. Heat the olive oil in another frying pan and fry the mushrooms for 3 minutes, stirring well. Add the spring onions and hazelnuts and cook for a further 1 minute.

5 Strain any liquid from the rice and then stir in the mushrooms. Season with salt and pepper to taste and serve.

Grilled Polenta (S)

Polenta is coarse yellow maize grain and is one of the staples of northern Italy where it often replaces bread. A couple of slices of grilled polenta with Star-gazer Vegetable Soup and a hearty salad make a well-balanced and satisfying lunch. It is also delicious with Stoved Mixed Mushrooms.

INGREDIENTS

Serves 4

900ml/1½ pints/3¾ cups water
175g/6oz/1¼ cups polenta
25g/1oz/2 tbsp butter
5ml/1 tsp extra virgin olive oil
salt and freshly ground black pepper

1 Boil the water in a large heavy-based saucepan and add 5ml/1 tsp salt. Reduce the heat until the water is just simmering and slowly pour in the polenta, stirring vigorously until completely blended.

2 Reduce the heat further and cook for 40 minutes, stirring every 5 minutes with a wooden spoon. The polenta is cooked when it is very thick and falls away from the sides of the pan.

3 Stir in the butter and seasoning and transfer to a flat baking sheet. Spread out until about 2.5cm/1in thick and set aside until completely cold.

4 Cut the polenta into wedges or slices and brush each piece lightly with olive oil. Place under a hot grill until each slice is crisp and brown on both sides. Serve hot.

Lentil Risotto with Vegetables (S)

INGREDIENTS

Serves 4

45ml/3 tbsp sunflower oil
1 large onion, thinly sliced
2 garlic cloves, crushed
1 large carrot, cut into matchsticks
225g/8oz/1 generous cup brown
  basmati rice, washed and drained
115g/4oz/½ cup green or brown
  lentils, soaked overnight and drained
5ml/1 tsp ground cumin
5ml/1 tsp ground cinnamon
20 black cardamom seeds
6 cloves
600ml/1 pint/2½ cups vegetable stock
2 bay leaves
2 celery sticks
1 large avocado
3 plum tomatoes
salt and freshly ground black pepper
green salad, to serve

1 Heat the oil in a heavy-based pan and fry the onion, garlic and carrot for 5–6 minutes, until the onion is transparent and the carrot is slightly softened.

2 Add the drained rice and lentils together with the cumin, cinnamon, cardamom seeds and cloves and continue frying over a low heat for a further 5 minutes, stirring well to prevent sticking.

3 Add the stock and bay leaves and bring to the boil, then cover the pan and simmer very gently for a further 15 minutes or until the liquid has been absorbed and the rice and lentils are tender. Taste and adjust the seasoning.

4 Meanwhile, chop the celery into half-rounds and dice the avocado and tomatoes.

5 Add the fresh ingredients to the rice and lentils and stir to mix. Spoon into a large serving bowl and serve immediately with a green salad.

Bean Feast with Tomato and Avocado Salsa (S)

This is a super-quick recipe using canned beans, although it could be made with dried beans, which would need to be soaked overnight and then cooked for 1–1½ hours until tender.

INGREDIENTS

Serves 4

400g/14oz can red kidney beans
400g/14oz can flageolet beans
400g/14oz can borlotti beans
15ml/1 tbsp olive oil
1 small onion, finely chopped
3 garlic cloves, finely chopped
1 red Ancho chilli, seeded and
    finely chopped
1 red pepper, seeded and
    coarsely chopped
2 bay leaves
10ml/2 tsp chopped fresh oregano
10ml/2 tsp ground cumin
5ml/1 tsp ground coriander
2.5ml/½ tsp ground cloves
15ml/1 tbsp dark brown sugar
300ml/½ pint/1¼ cups vegetable stock
salt and freshly ground black pepper
sprigs of fresh coriander, to garnish

For the salsa

1 ripe but firm avocado
45ml/3 tbsp fresh lime juice
1 small red onion
1 small hot green chilli
3 ripe plum tomatoes
45ml/3 tbsp chopped fresh coriander

1 Drain the beans in a colander and rinse thoroughly. Heat the oil in a heavy-based saucepan and fry the onion for 3 minutes, until soft and transparent. Add the garlic, chilli, red pepper, herbs and spices.

2 Stir well and cook for a further 3 minutes, then add the sugar, beans and stock and cook for 8 minutes. Season with salt and pepper.

3 To make the salsa, peel the avocado, cut it in half around the stone, then remove the stone using a large sharp knife. Cut the flesh into 1cm/½ in dice. Place in a mixing bowl with the lime juice and stir to mix.

4 Roughly chop the onion and finely slice the chilli, discarding the seeds. Plunge the tomatoes into boiling water, leave for 1 minute and then peel away the skin. Chop the tomatoes into rough pieces and discard the seeds.

5 Add the onion, chilli, tomatoes and coriander to the avocado. Season with black pepper and stir to mix.

6 Spoon the beans into a warmed serving dish or into four serving bowls. Serve with the tomato and avocado salsa and garnish with sprigs of fresh coriander.

PASTA AND PASTRY

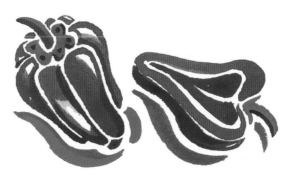

Pasta or gnocchi makes a filling starch meal especially when combined with one of the different and original sauces included here. The sauces can also be served with brown rice or spooned over split baked potatoes or lightly steamed vegetables. While making pastry with wholewheat flour is recommended, it does no harm to your diet to occasionally use the ready-made, light and super-thin filo pastry, especially when it is filled with plenty of tasty Mediterranean vegetables or used to envelop a subtle combination of cream cheese, leeks and fresh herbs.

Chinese Primavera (S)

INGREDIENTS

Serves 4

350g/12oz capellini pasta (egg-free)
2.5ml/½ tsp salt
15ml/1 tbsp groundnut oil
1 red pepper, seeded
1 yellow pepper, seeded
115g/4oz/1 cup mangetouts
10 button mushrooms
3 spring onions
30ml/2 tbsp cornflour
15ml/1 tbsp olive oil
3 garlic cloves, finely chopped
175ml/6fl oz/¾ cup vegetable stock
45ml/3 tbsp dry sherry
30ml/2 tbsp sesame oil
15ml/1 tbsp light soy sauce
5ml/1 tsp chilli sauce
15ml/1 tbsp oyster sauce
2.5ml/½ tsp caster sugar
2.5ml/½ tsp Szechuan peppercorns,
   crushed
rind of 1 orange, cut into thin shreds,
   to garnish

1 Place the pasta in a large pan of boiling water with the salt and cook for 3 minutes. Drain in a colander and then transfer to a large bowl and stir in the groundnut oil.

COOK'S TIP

Capellini, vermicelli or angel hair pasta cooks very quickly and is ideal for quick meals. Serve with slices of fresh tomato sprinkled with chopped basil leaves and a little extra virgin olive oil.

2 Cut the peppers into matchsticks, halve the mangetouts, thinly slice the mushrooms and shred the spring onions. Stir them into the pasta.

3 Blend the cornflour with 30ml/ 2 tbsp water in a small bowl.

4 Heat the olive oil in a wok and stir-fry the garlic for 20 seconds. Add the vegetable stock, sherry, sesame oil, soy, chilli and oyster sauces, sugar and peppercorns. Bring to the boil and pour in the cornflour mixture, stirring all the time.

5 Add the pasta and vegetables and heat through for 2 minutes. Serve at once, garnished with orange rind.

Black Pasta with Raw Vegetables (S)

Black pasta derives its dramatic colour from the addition of squid ink. Alternatively you could use Japanese soba or buckwheat noodles, which have a nutty flavour and texture.

INGREDIENTS

Serves 4

3 garlic cloves, crushed
30ml/2 tbsp white tarragon vinegar
5ml/1 tsp Dijon mustard
90ml/6 tbsp extra virgin olive oil
5ml/1 tsp finely chopped fresh thyme
1 yellow pepper, seeded
1 red pepper, seeded
225g/8oz mangetouts, topped
  and tailed
6 radishes
4 ripe plum tomatoes, peeled
  and seeded
1 avocado
salt and freshly ground black pepper
275g/10oz black pasta (egg-free)
6 fresh basil leaves, to garnish

1 In a large bowl, blend together the garlic, vinegar, mustard, olive oil and chopped thyme. Season to taste with salt and pepper.

2 Cut the peppers into diamond shapes, halve the mangetouts and slice the radishes.

3 Dice the tomatoes. Peel, stone and slice the avocado. Place all the vegetables in a bowl and add the dressing, stirring thoroughly to mix.

4 Cook the pasta in plenty of slightly salted boiling water until *al dente*. The cooking time will vary depending on the type of pasta. Drain and tip into a large shallow serving dish. Cover with the vegetables and serve immediately, garnished with basil leaves.

Courgette and Dill Tart (S)

It is worth making your own pastry for this tart. Although shop-bought shortcrust pastry is a useful standby, it never tastes quite as good as home-made.

INGREDIENTS

Serves 4
115g/4oz/1 cup plain
   wholemeal flour
115g/4oz/1 cup self-raising flour
115g/4oz/8 tbsp unsalted butter,
   chilled and diced
75ml/5 tbsp ice-cold water
pinch salt

For the filling
15ml/1 tbsp sunflower oil
3 courgettes, thinly sliced
2 egg yolks
150ml/¼ pint/⅔ cup double cream
1 garlic clove, crushed
15ml/1 tbsp finely chopped fresh dill
salt and freshly ground black pepper

1 Sift the flours into a bowl, returning any of the wheat bran into the bowl, then place in a food processor. Add the salt and butter and process using the pulse button until the mixture resembles fine breadcrumbs.

2 Gradually add the water until the mixture forms a dough. Do not over process. Rest the pastry by wrapping it in clear cling film and placing in the fridge for 30 minutes.

3 Preheat the oven to 200°C/400°F/ Gas 6 and grease a 20cm/8in flan tin. Roll out the pastry and ease into the tin. Prick the base with a fork and bake "blind" for 10-15 minutes until lightly browned.

4 Meanwhile heat the oil in a frying pan and sauté the courgettes for 2–3 minutes until lightly browned, turning occasionally. Blend the egg yolks, double cream, garlic and dill in a small bowl. Season to taste with salt and pepper.

5 Line the pastry case with layers of courgette and gently pour over the cream mixture. Return to the oven for 25–30 minutes or until the filling is firm and lightly golden. Cool in the tin and then remove and serve.

Potato Gnocchi with Fresh Tomato Sauce (S)

Gnocchi make a substantial and tasty alternative to pasta. They are served with a fresh tomato sauce, which, because the tomatoes are simply warmed through for a short time, and not cooked, remains neutral.

INGREDIENTS

Serves 4

675g/1½lb potatoes, floury type
2 egg yolks
75g/3oz/¾ cup plain flour
salt
60ml/4 tbsp finely chopped fresh
    parsley, to garnish

For the sauce
450g/1lb plum tomatoes, peeled,
    seeded and chopped
30ml/2 tbsp melted butter

1 Preheat the oven to 200°C/400°F/ Gas 6. Scrub the potatoes and bake in their jackets in the oven for 1 hour or until the flesh feels soft when pricked with a fork.

2 Peel the potatoes while still warm, discarding the skins, and mash the flesh well. Add a little salt and stir in the egg yolks.

3 Place the potato mixture on a floured surface and knead in the flour to make a smooth elastic dough.

4 Shape the dough into small thumb–shapes by making long rolls and cutting them into segments. Press each gnocchi with the back of a fork to give a ridged effect. Place the gnocchi on a floured surface.

5 Cook the gnocchi in small batches in barely simmering, slightly salted water for about 10 minutes. Remove with a slotted spoon, drain well and keep warm.

6 To make the sauce, cook the tomatoes in the butter in a small pan for 1 minute. Sprinkle the gnocchi with chopped parsley and serve at once with the sauce.

Sunflower and Almond Sesame Crackers (N)

One thing food combiners often yearn for is cheese and biscuits at the end of a meal. These neutral crackers can be served either with your favourite cheese or as a base for fish or meat canapés.

INGREDIENTS

Makes about 24

130g/4½oz/1 cup ground sunflower seeds
90g/3½oz/¾ cup ground almonds
5ml/1 tsp baking powder
30ml/2 tbsp milk
1 egg yolk
25g/1oz/2 tbsp butter, melted
25g/1oz/¼ cup sesame seeds

1 Preheat the oven to 190°C/375°F/ Gas 5. Reserve 25g/1oz/¼ cup of the ground sunflower seeds for rolling out, and mix the remaining ground seeds with the ground almonds and baking powder in a bowl.

2 Blend together the milk and egg yolk and stir into the ground seed and almond mixture with the melted butter, mixing well. Gently work the mixture with your hands to form a moist dough.

—— VARIATION ——

Sprinkle some poppy seeds on top of a few of the biscuits before baking.

3 Roll out the dough to about 5mm/¼in thickness on a cool surface, lightly dusted with a little of the reserved ground sunflower seeds, with a little more sprinkled on top to prevent sticking.

4 Sprinkle the dough with sesame seeds and cut into rounds using a 5cm/2in pastry cutter. Lift on to a non-stick baking sheet.

5 Bake the crackers for about 10 minutes until lightly browned. Cool on a wire rack.

DESSERTS

Desserts don't have to be wicked to be wonderful and a small indulgence does no harm, particularly when it is made from the very best ingredients. When you are planning a menu, remember to match protein desserts with protein main courses and starch desserts with starch main courses. All the recipes are simple to make, and desserts such as Stem Ginger Ice Cream, Passion Fruit Brûlée and Soft Fruit Pavlova are perfect for entertaining, while Pear and Cardamom Sponge will appeal to everyone and could be served at any family celebration.

Sweet Pear and Cardamom Sponge (S)

Choose very sweet dessert pears, like Comice or Williams, for this delicious dessert. They need to be completely ripe and very juicy. Serve with a dollop of whipped cream or ice cream.

INGREDIENTS

Serves 4

5 pears
10 green cardamom pods
115g/4oz/1 cup self-raising flour
5ml/1 tsp baking powder
115g/4oz/generous ½ cup caster sugar
115g/4oz/½ cup butter, softened
3 egg yolks
30–45ml/2–3 tbsp warm water

1 Preheat the oven to 190°C/375°F/ Gas 5. Line the base of a 20cm/8in diameter cake tin with greaseproof paper and then butter and lightly flour the sides.

2 Peel the pears, cut them in half and remove the cores. Lay the fruit cut side up in a circle in the bottom of the prepared tin.

3 Remove the cardamom seeds from the pods and crush the seeds lightly using a pestle and mortar.

4 Sift together the flour and baking powder. Add the sugar, crushed cardamom seeds, butter, egg yolks and 30ml/2 tbsp of the water. Beat with an electric or hand whisk until creamy. The mixture should fall off a spoon; if it does not, add a little more water.

5 Place the mixture on top of the pears and level with a knife. Bake for 45–50 minutes until the cake is firm.

6 Turn the cake out on to a wire rack and peel off the greaseproof paper. Cool before serving.

Stem Ginger Ice Cream (N)

This rich and flavourful ice cream goes beautifully with sliced fresh pears and bananas at the end of a starch meal or with gooseberry and apple purée after a protein main course.

INGREDIENTS

Serves 4
15ml/1 tbsp clear honey
4 egg yolks
600ml/1 pint/2½ cups double cream, lightly whipped
4 pieces of preserved stem ginger, chopped into tiny dice

1 Place the honey and 150ml/¼ pint/ ²⁄₃ cup water in a small saucepan and heat until the honey is completely dissolved. Remove from the heat and allow to cool.

2 Place the egg yolks in a large bowl and whisk gently until pale and frothy. Slowly add the honey syrup and fold in the whipped cream.

3 Pour the mixture into a plastic freezer container and freeze for about 45 minutes or until the ice cream is freezing at the edges.

4 Transfer to a bowl and whisk again. Mix in the stem ginger, reserving a few pieces for decoration. Freeze again for 2–4 hours. Serve the ice cream in scoops, decorated with the reserved stem ginger.

—— COOK'S TIP ——

Transfer the ice cream from the freezer to the fridge 20 minutes before serving.

Passion Fruit Brûlée (P)

Fruit brûlées are usually made with double cream, but thick yogurt, which has a rich flavour and is more easily digested, works equally well. The brown sugar required for this recipe is reserved for the crunchy caramelized topping as the passion fruit pulp is naturally very sweet.

INGREDIENTS

Serves 4
4 passion fruit
300ml/½ pint/1¼ cups Greek or thick natural yogurt
75g/3oz/½ cup soft light brown sugar

1 Cut the passion fruit in half using a very sharp knife. Use a teaspoon to scoop out all the pulp and seeds and divide equally between four small ovenproof ramekins.

2 Spoon equal amounts of the yogurt on top of the fruit and smooth the surface until it is completely flat and level. Chill for at least 2 hours.

3 Place the sugar in a small saucepan with 15ml/1 tbsp water and heat gently until the sugar has melted and caramelized. Pour over the yogurt: the caramel will harden within 1 minute. Keep the brûlées in a cool place until ready to serve.

Grilled Nectarines with Amaretto (P)

Amaretto, the sweet almond-flavoured liqueur from Italy, adds a touch of luxury to many soft fruits, particularly peaches and nectarines. Enhance the nutty taste by scattering some lightly toasted flaked almonds, still hot from the grill, on top of the crème fraîche just before serving.

INGREDIENTS

Serves 4
6 ripe nectarines
30ml/2 tbsp clear honey
60ml/4 tbsp Amaretto
crème fraîche, to serve

1 Cut the nectarines in half by running a small sharp knife down the side of each fruit from top to bottom, pushing the knife right through to the stone. Gently ease the nectarine apart and remove the stone.

2 Place the nectarines cut side up in an ovenproof dish and drizzle about 2.5ml/½ tsp honey and 5ml/1 tsp Amaretto over each half.

3 Preheat the grill until very hot and then grill the fruit for a few minutes until slightly charred. Arrange the nectarine halves on four small serving plates and serve with a little crème fraîche.

Honey Almond Cream (N)

This dessert is best served after a light main course as it is very rich and deliciously indulgent. Serve with seasonal soft berries such as blueberries, raspberries or blackberries after a protein meal. Alternatively serve with slices of very sweet fresh pears or bananas after a starch main course.

INGREDIENTS

Serves 4
275g/10oz/1¼ cups cream cheese or mascarpone
50g/2oz/½ cup ground almonds
1 egg yolk
15ml/1 tbsp clear honey
tiny drop of vanilla essence
50ml/2fl oz/¼ cup double cream
fresh fruit, to serve

1 Line a 10cm/4in new or well-scrubbed terracotta flowerpot with fine muslin, allowing a generous overhang around the sides.

2 Blend together the cheese and ground almonds in a bowl.

— VARIATION —

A small handful of sultanas or raisins can be added to the cheese mixture, if liked.

3 Beat the egg yolk and honey together in another bowl and add the vanilla essence.

4 Lightly whip the cream, fold it into the cheese mixture and stir carefully until the mixture has the consistency of thick mayonnaise. Add the egg and honey and mix gently.

5 Spoon into the flower pot and fold over the muslin to cover. Place a small weighted plate on the top.

6 Stand the flowerpot in a dish to catch any excess liquid and place in the fridge overnight. When ready to serve, carefully turn out on to a plate and serve with the fresh fruit.

Soft Fruit Pavlova (P)

There is a lot of sugar in meringue, but for special occasions this is the queen of desserts and a practical way of using up egg whites left over after making ice cream or mayonnaise.

INGREDIENTS

Serves 4

4 egg whites
175g/6oz/1¼ cups caster sugar
30ml/2 tbsp redcurrant jelly
300ml/½ pint/1¼ cups double cream, whipped, or crème fraîche
15ml/1 tbsp rose water
450g/1lb mixed soft fruits, such as blackberries, blueberries, redcurrants, raspberries or loganberries
10ml/2 tsp sifted icing sugar
pinch of salt

1 Preheat the oven to 140°C/275°F/ Gas 1. Oil a baking sheet. Whisk the egg whites with a pinch of salt in a spotlessly clean bowl, until they are white and stiff. Slowly add the sugar and keep whisking until the mixture makes stiff, glossy peaks.

--- COOK'S TIP ---

Meringues may be made in advance and stored in an airtight tin or better still kept in the freezer.

2 Spoon the meringue into a 25cm/10in round on the baking sheet, making a slight indentation in the centre and soft crests around the outside. Bake for 1–1½ hours until the meringue is firm. Keep checking as the meringue can easily overcook and turn brown. Transfer the meringue to a serving plate.

3 Melt the redcurrant jelly in a small bowl resting in a pan of hot water. Cool slightly, then spread the jelly in the centre of the meringue.

4 Gently mix the rose water with the whipped cream or crème fraîche and spoon into the centre of the meringue. Arrange the fruits on top and dust lightly with icing sugar.

Papaya and Green Grapes with Mint Syrup (S)

Papaya is rich in vitamins A, C and E and also contains calcium, phosphorus and iron. It is very easily digested and has a tonic effect on the stomach, so makes the perfect dessert to follow a richly flavoured starch course, such as Filo Baskets with Mediterranean Vegetables.

INGREDIENTS

Serves 4
2 large papaya
225g/8oz seedless green grapes
juice of 3 limes
2.5cm/1in fresh root ginger, peeled
   and finely grated
15ml/1 tbsp clear honey
5 fresh mint leaves, cut into thin strips,
   plus extra whole leaves, to decorate

1 Peel the papaya and cut into small cubes, discarding the seeds. Cut the grapes in half.

2 In a bowl, mix together the lime juice, ginger, honey and shredded mint leaves.

3 Add the papaya and grapes and toss well. Leave in a cool place to marinate for 1 hour.

4 Serve in a large dish or individual stemmed glasses, garnished with whole fresh mint leaves.

Orange Granita with Strawberries (P)

Granita is a crunchy sorbet that is simple to make and requires no special equipment. Use very juicy oranges and really ripe strawberries that do not need any additional sweetening.

INGREDIENTS

Serves 4
6 large juicy oranges
350g/12oz ripe strawberries
finely pared strips of orange rind,
   to decorate

COOK'S TIP

Granita will keep for up to 3 weeks in the freezer. Sweet pink grapefruits or deep red blood oranges can be used for a different flavour and colour. Add a little fresh lemon juice if you prefer a more tart ice.

1 Squeeze the juice from the oranges and pour into a shallow freezer-proof bowl.

2 Place the bowl in the freezer. Remove after 30 minutes and beat the semi-frozen juice thoroughly with a wooden spoon. Repeat this process at 30-minute intervals over a 4-hour period. This will break the ice crystals down into small particles. Halve the strawberries and arrange them on a serving plate. Scoop the granita into serving glasses, decorate with strips of orange rind and serve immediately with the strawberries.

INDEX